CONTENTS

Hc 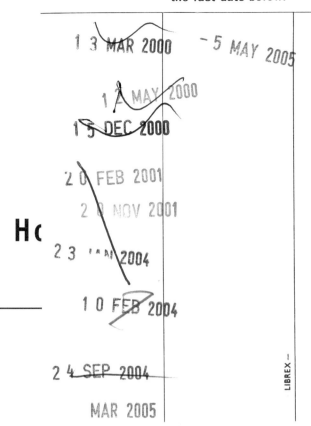 th:

and L

The Chartered Institute of Housing
The Chartered Institute of Housing is the professional organisation for everyone who works in housing. Its purpose is to take a strategic and leading role in encouraging and promoting the provision of good quality, affordable housing for all. The Institute has more than 14,000 members working in local authorities, housing associations, the private sector and educational institutions.

Chartered Institute of Housing
Octavia House
Westwood Way
Coventry CV4 8JP
Tel: 01203 851700
Fax: 01203 695110

The Local Government Association
The Local Government Association represents local authorities in England and Wales. Its main purpose is to present the case for local government. As the national voice for local communities, it speaks for nearly 500 local authorities representing over 50 million people and spending £65 billion a year on local services.

The Local Government Association
26 Chapter Street
London SW1P 4ND
Tel: 0171 834 2222
Fax: 0171 834 2263

Housing Strategies for Youth
Written by Kate Folkard
Commissioning Editor: Sarah Edwards
Editor: Steve Platt

© Chartered Institute of Housing and Local Government Association, April 1998
Published by the Chartered Institute of Housing and the Local Government Association
ISBN 1 900396 07 6

Design by Jeremy Spencer
Cover illustration by Liz Pichon
Printed by Hobbs the Printers, Totton

List of principal boxes

FOREWORD

A Message from the Minister for Local Government and Housing

Addressing the housing needs of young people is a complex process that rests on a range of statutory requirements and voluntary provisions. It calls for inputs from a range of players. Many of the best approaches have been developed as local responses to particular needs by those with front line experience of working with young people. I particularly welcome this Good Practice Guide because it brings together a wealth of material and best practice into a single work of reference.

Equally, the way in which it has been produced, as a partnership between members of the voluntary sector (Centrepoint), the housing profession (the Chartered Institute of Housing) and the statutory authorities (the Local Government Association), gives a good example of the sort of joint working that is so important in tackling youth homelessness. There is something in this guide for those working in all these fields.

Youth homelessness can be a terrible personal tragedy and blight a young person's chances at the start of his or her career. We must all work together towards its eradication. This guide makes a valuable contribution to that process.

Hilary Armstrong MP

ABOUT THE AUTHOR

Kate Folkard is the policy and development officer at Centrepoint, the youth homelessness organisation, with responsibility for policy analysis, good practice advice and the management of the external training programme. She is currently studying for a Masters in Housing at the London School of Economics.

Before joining Centrepoint, Kate worked at the Housing Corporation on the review of special needs funding. She has also worked as an outreach worker for a voluntary youth project in Cambridge, where she developed housing advocacy work for 16 and 17-year-olds.

Kate started her working life in Sheffield with an extensive range of voluntary work, including work with people who are homeless. While in Sheffield she developed housing education work for schools and youth clubs.

Centrepoint
Central Office
Bewlay House
2 Swallow Place
London W1R 7AA
Tel: 0171 544 5000
Fax: 0171 544 5001

ABOUT THE SPONSORS

The Chartered Institute of Housing, the Local Government Association and Centrepoint would like to acknowledge the generous sponsorship of a number of organisations whose support has made this publication possible.

Major sponsors:
> The Housing Corporation
> North British Housing Association

Other sponsoring organisations:
> HACAS
> Leicester Housing Association
> Charnwood Forest Housing Association

ACKNOWLEDGEMENTS

My thanks are due to many people for their help in producing this guide, including Sarah Edwards, of the Chartered Institute of Housing, as the commissioning editor, Geoff Matthews, of the Local Government Association, and Steve Platt, who edited the manuscript.

I am sincerely grateful to all those who provided information about their organisations, which illustrate the guide vividly. Also to the steering group who read the drafts of the guide and provided valuable comments, particularly:

Dan Finn, University of Portsmouth
Simon Inkson, City and County of Swansea
Matthew Waters, Shelter
Martin Hazelhurst, First Key
Laurie Naumann, Scottish Council for Single Homeless
Howard Williamson, University of Wales
Tamsin Stirling, Chartered Institute of Housing in Wales
Amanda Allard, NCH Action for Children
Jill Tufnell, Cambridgeshire County Council
Philippa O'Neill, National Housing Federation
Stewart Betts, Norfolk Social Services
Gilda Costley, South Herefordshire District Council
Jo Lavis, Rural Development Commission
Simeon Brody, National Homeless Alliance
Marian Reid, Chartered Institute of Housing in Scotland
Jane Haywood, Department for Education and Employment

For additional comments and information, thanks are due to Bill Payne of Yorkshire Metropolitan Housing Association, Steve Town of the DETR, John Nelson of the DfEE and Mags Alison of Shelter. Duncan Forbes and James Bauld contributed invaluable legal comment.

Many thanks to my colleagues at Centrepoint, particularly Cathy Havell, Jeremy Spafford, Henrietta Yannaghas and to Radhika Holmstrom.

And finally for the support I received from Naisha Polaine, Lucia Limb and Stella Smith.

Kate Folkard, Centrepoint

CHAPTER 1

Introduction

☐ The context

Everyone needs a secure place to live. Young people, who are going through the difficult transition to independent living, need one particularly. Yet many do not have the necessary income, contacts, knowledge or experience to obtain and maintain an adequate home.

Young people's housing options are limited. Home ownership is out of reach for most of them, while a declining social rented stock (the number of local authority homes in the UK fell from 6.57 million in 1981 to 4.87 million in 1994) has resulted in access being restricted to the minority who are covered by a very strict interpretation of homelessness legislation. Housing associations still only account for about four per cent of homes. Many of their developments, moreover, consist primarily of family housing, reflecting the statutory obligations placed on local authorities. Young, single people have found themselves squeezed.

Even in the private rented sector, which has expanded by some 300,000 homes since rent deregulation in 1988, access for many young people has narrowed. Restrictions on the availability of housing and other benefits, in particular, have had a major impact. Since 1996, most single people aged under 25 have had their housing benefit restricted to the 'single room rent' level; they also receive a lower rate of Jobseeker's Allowance. Benefits for 16 and 17-year-olds are even more tightly restricted.

☐ Purpose of the Guide

This Guide provides good practice advice on housing young people. It sets out the framework for professionals working with young people in housing need, and details the support and provision that young people may require in their move towards independence. Since no one agency can provide the full range of services an individual requires for a successful transition to independence, a strategic approach is essential to meeting those needs efficiently and effectively. The Guide outlines the elements of a successful strategic approach.

Publication coincides with the launch of the government's 'New Deal' on training and employment for young people. This provides an opportunity to rethink housing strategies for young people in a broader context, across the whole range of agencies involved. Young people's needs must be addressed in a holistic way; agencies with a range of skills and expertise need to come together. The government recognises this in encouraging partnerships between agencies to deliver the New Deal. This approach will not succeed, however, unless young people's accommodation needs form a central plank of the New Deal process. The Employment Service does not have the expertise to deal with accommodation needs and is actively seeking the support of local partners such as housing organisations.

It is also important that young people themselves are involved in the planning and delivery of services designed for them, ensuring that they are appropriate and relevant. Throughout this Guide, therefore, the involvement of young people is accorded a central role.

The Guide focuses on the issues that are particularly relevant to young people. It aims to complement existing publications and does not unnecessarily duplicate material that is available elsewhere. Because it covers such a wide range of topics, it is not possible to explore all issues in detail or to provide comprehensive reports of the specific projects mentioned. Additional information can be obtained via the appendix listing References and further reading.

Terminology

The term 'young people' is used to refer to those aged 16-24.

Appropriate references are made to the legislation of the different countries in the UK. Where the generic terms 'Children Act' and 'Housing Act' are used, these should be taken as referring collectively to the Children Act 1989, the Children (Scotland) Act 1995 and the Children (Northern Ireland) Order 1995; and the Housing Act 1996, the Housing (Scotland) Act 1987, the Housing (Scotland) Act 1988 and the Housing (Northern Ireland) Order 1988 respectively.

Where other housing acts are referred to their titles are given in full.

CHAPTER 2

A Plan for Success:
Developing a Strategic Approach

☐ Introduction

Organising activity across such diverse sectors as housing, social services, health, education and employment is a complex task, but real improvements in young people's housing options require thorough planning. A strategy to tackle local problems must start with the views of young people and those who work with them. Agencies must combine resources to implement that strategy.

This chapter explores the strategic process and joint working. It sets out why it is necessary to work in such a way, how to do so successfully and who should be involved. It also covers the basic principles and methods of involving young people.

☐ The strategic process

What is the strategic process?

A strategy is really no more than a 'plan for success'. It involves identifying a problem accurately and devising the means by which it can be tackled. It needs, therefore, to be realistic, and for the people who are responsible for implementing it to feel that they 'own' it. It should be developed and delivered by a range of organisations and individuals, and provision should be made for regular review and amendment in the light of experience.

The strategic process consists of four stages: audit and research; strategy; development and implementation; and evaluation.

The **audit and research** stage involves, first, assessing needs and, second, carrying out an audit of existing services.

The **strategy** will identify what developments are required in policy, practice, training, awareness raising and new services. It will also determine which of these areas are a priority, where the resources are, what partnerships are necessary and which agency should lead. Priorities can be identified by a number of methods, as long as these are adhered to systematically.

Development and implementation of the strategy should take into account the different agencies' capacity to take on new work, and the support they need.

In order to **evaluate** the process, appropriate **monitoring systems** need to be in place.

Why develop a strategic approach?

The report of the national inquiry into preventing youth homelessness led by CHAR (Evans, 1996) made the case that there is an urgent need for a more strategic and coordinated approach to the housing needs of young people: "Without an over-arching plan or strategy there is no guarantee that the most urgent needs of young people are being met. There can be unnecessary and wasteful duplication of services and difficulties for young people in finding their way around the bewildering maze of different organisations." CHAR's guide to developing single homelessness strategies (McCluskey, 1997) shows that where they have been adopted, such strategies have made a significant impact, resulting in increased or improved provision, better services, improved inter-agency working, better coordination, more available information, changes in policy and procedures, better use of existing resources and access to additional funding.

A strategic approach is, in fact, a government requirement. Local authorities must publish a statement summarising the key elements of their housing strategy; and one of the objectives of the Housing Investment Programme process is to encourage authorities to take a strategic approach to their housing responsibilities (Department of the Environment, 1995). The revised Codes of Guidance on Parts VI and VII of the Housing Act 1996, which are due to be published in England and Wales in mid-1998, will also remind local authorities of their responsibilities to single people. These are expected to encourage authorities to take a broad strategic view of their responsibilities and to emphasise the importance of joint working.

A strategy addressing the needs of young people is particularly necessary because of differences between the Housing Act and Children Act. The codes of guidance attached to the Housing Act 1996 and Housing (Scotland) Act 1987 explicitly require housing and social services departments to work together (see chapter 5 for more details).

Youth housing strategies must also link in with other relevant strategies, in areas such as single homelessness, children's service, community care, anti-poverty, local planning and New Deal delivery. It is particularly important to integrate strategic approaches to housing young people with the local housing strategy to ensure that young people's housing needs are not marginalised. Regional strategies may also be useful in areas where one local authority (covering a city centre, for example) attracts single homeless people from a wider area. (See Goss and Blackaby (1998) for more details on integrating strategy.)

Southern Health and Social Services Board Area, Northern Ireland: An inter-agency strategy on youth homelessness

In 1996, a report, *Meeting the Need: An inter-agency approach to understanding and responding to youth homelessness*, was published. Commissioned by the Southern Health and Social Services Board, the Probation Board NI and the NI Housing Executive, and carried out by the Simon Community NI, it assessed local need in the light of the impending implementation of the Children (NI) Order. It also identified the amount, type and level of current provision, making suggestions and recommendations as to how to close the gaps and meet needs. Young people in the area who were or had been homeless were consulted.

Bradford: A multi-agency consortium that links in with a number of other local authority strategies and forums

Bradford Young Persons Housing Consortium was established in 1992 to coordinate services and develop policies. The consortium was developed in response to a shortage of accommodation for single homeless young people and has facilitated the development of more than 100 new units of supported housing. It is coordinated by the local authority, which seconded an officer from the housing directorate.

The consortium operates as a reference group for both Bradford Housing Forum, which coordinates and develops the local authority housing strategy, and the working party on homelessness, which in turn feeds in to the integrated children's service plan. It is also in contact with youth forums, which focus on preventative mediation work, and the support group for a city centre housing project. In June 1997, Bradford Housing Forum sponsored a conference, which involved young people, to develop a young people's housing strategy. Interested parties are currently being consulted on the resulting strategic document.

☐ Joint working

Although individual organisations can develop their own internal strategies, a joint youth homelessness strategy is much more effective. Indeed, "the very essence of the enabling housing authority is its capacity to pull together the myriad resources of public sector, voluntary sector and private sector organisations to meet local housing needs" (Malpass and Means, 1993).

It is important not to confuse the concepts of strategic working and joint working, although they often go hand in hand. Each organisation should have its own individual strategy. It is also important to remember that joint working does not just take place at the planning stage, but is equally important during delivery, when agencies with differing expertise will come together to provide a service.

Shelter/Essex probation service: Two agencies with different expertise working together to provide a service

Essex probation service has a contract with Shelter's housing advice centre in Colchester to provide expert housing advice to probation clients. The contract is financed by Home Office partnership funding and stipulates the employment of one full-time adviser. The adviser is available every morning to provide advice and visits each of the five probation offices for one afternoon every two weeks. He also attends probation service accommodation officers' team meetings and provides training and policy briefings.

Cases are referred to the adviser via accommodation officers rather than directly from probation officers. This ensures that accommodation officers deal with standard inquiries and only refer clients on when expert advice is needed. This arrangement has proved crucial for two reasons. First, it ensures an efficient use of resources and expertise. Second, the presence of accommodation officers in each probation office, dealing with securing accommodation and general housing issues, helps probation officers to realise the importance of housing in their work.

Why develop a multi-agency approach?

In general, multi-agency working is valuable for several reasons, as detailed below. There may also be additional value for organisations working in a particular field — see Watson and Conway (1995), for instance, for more details in relation to community care.

- **A coherent service for young people:** The aim should be to provide as 'seamless' a service as possible. This can only be achieved through joint working. Joint working also ensures that the 'revolving door' syndrome is avoided and that the young person is treated consistently wherever they first present themselves.

- **A common understanding of the issue:** Professionals from different agencies who deal with young people have been trained in a variety of disciplines, work in differing organisational cultures and have diverse experiences. Bringing these perspectives together can be very valuable, although it is also crucial to acknowledge differences and reach an agreed definition and understanding of the issue.

- **An assessment of the local situation from a range of perspectives:** Each agency will have a very different view of the local situation, based on the type of work they do. In order to get a comprehensive picture, agencies must draw together their information and experience (see chapter 3 for more details).

- **Pooled information, expertise and experience:** No one agency can be expected to understand all the issues in depth. By bringing together their differing perspectives agencies can draw on a wider range of knowledge and expertise.

- **No unnecessary duplication of services:** If agencies are working together to improve services, it will prevent different organisations duplicating provision.

- **Increased effectiveness in attracting resources to the area:** Many funders require local partnerships. Even where this is not the case, an application based on a thorough multi-agency assessment of need and provision is likely to be more successful than an application made by one agency in isolation. Many sources of funds are also only available to one sector. By working together on a project agencies can increase their access to funding.

Agencies involved in joint working

A wide range of organisations should be involved in joint work. Each of these can make their own contribution to the process and gain from it themselves:

- Housing departments
- Social services departments
- Youth service

- Education departments
- Schools, sixth-form and further education colleges
- Economic development unit
- Health service
- Advice agencies
- Young people's information shops
- Housing Corporation/Tai Cymru/Scottish Homes/Northern Ireland Housing Executive
- Accommodation providers, including housing associations
- Voluntary agencies
- Training and Enterprise Councils and Local Enterprise Companies
- Employment Service
- Trade unions
- Careers service
- Benefits Agency
- Housing benefit office
- Police
- Probation service
- Church groups

This is not an exhaustive list, but it does cover the main organisations that might be partners in a young people's housing strategy. It is also good practice to involve young people themselves (see below for more detail).

Multi-agency forums

In order to work together successfully, it is important that agencies meet at regular, although not necessarily frequent, intervals. This also enables people to get to know each other, which is often the most appreciated aspect of a multi-agency forum.

Obviously, different forums will have different aims and be at different stages of development. A forum's role will also be affected by the staff who attend — 'frontline' workers or policy-makers, for example. This will determine whether it should concentrate on improving service delivery within existing resource constraints or on long term strategic planning that is likely to require additional funding.

Multi-agency forums can fulfil a wide variety of functions:

- Sharing information and networking
- Supporting frontline or isolated workers
- Streamlining services and establishing common procedures
- Addressing the specific needs of young people who have been 'looked after' by the local authority
- Initiating joint training and staff development
- Monitoring the incidence of youth homelessness
- Developing a strategy to meet young people's housing, advice and support needs — prioritising and assigning lead responsibility for tasks and establishing an appropriate monitoring system

Difficulties of joint working

The multi-agency approach does have its problems. Initially, progress is likely to be slow, as agencies adjust to each other's perspectives and procedures. It may also be difficult to attract the right agencies to the forum, or ensure consistent attendance. Alternatively, an agency may attend regularly but send an inappropriate representative. At this early stage, it is difficult to maintain different members' levels of interest and commitment. However, as a forum becomes established and develops appropriate ways of working, a diary of meeting dates and clear responsibilities, this pressure will ease.

The culture of competition that sometimes permeates housing work can be fatal to collaborative multi-agency working. However, housing organisations also work in a culture of partnerships, and although most of the major sources of government funding have a competitive element, they do emphasise the need for organisations to work together.

Successful joint working

The difficulties of joint working can be tackled by:

- Clarity about a forum's purpose and stated aims
- Clear objectives and boundaries of a forum's responsibilities
- Sharing power, often in new and innovative ways that require trust between organisations
- Prioritising a forum's tasks. Tasks can be prioritised by various criteria, including importance and achievability. It may help in gaining

commitment and maintaining interest if some of the achievable tasks are completed relatively quickly. This will give a forum the impetus to tackle the important ones

- Clarity on where responsibilities lie, including timescales

- Explicit expectations of one another. This is particularly important when organisations of differing sizes and resources are involved. Unrealistic expectations should not be placed on small organisations

- Agency, not individual, commitment — to ensure that the commitment is not lost if an individual leaves

- Keeping agencies informed when they do not attend

- Ensuring appropriate representation from each agency. There is little value in a director of housing attending meetings to discuss the detail of a common referral form, while a frontline advice worker will have little to add to the detailed planning process of a new hostel.

- Acknowledging the culture of competition and deciding how to deal with it. For example, if the forum decides new accommodation is needed, will a number of housing associations bid competitively for it, will they form a development consortium, or will one association bid with the support of the others?

- Involving young people. It may be more appropriate to use a separate young people's forum, feeding information between the two groups, rather than to include young people in the agency forum. It may not be necessary to set up a new group solely for this purpose; there may be an existing young people's forum, such as a youth council, that can be consulted on housing issues.

☐ Involving young people

Involving young people from an early stage will help to avoid under-used services, management difficulties and the need for the major remodelling of projects. **Involvement** means that young people have opportunities to influence the policies and practice that affect them. Involvement can include both consultation and participation.

Consultation means that young people are asked their views, which will be taken into account when decisions are made. **Participation** means that young people can influence decision-making and take part in the decision-making process where ideas and information are shared. There are varying degrees of consultation and participation.

Box 2a: Arnstein's Ladder of Participation

7. Young people take all decisions

6. Young people take decisions about some aspects

5. Young people are able to influence decisions

4. Young people are consulted

3. Young people are informed of proposals

2. Young people are told of decisions made

1. Young people are ignored

Source: Arnstein, 1969

Principles of involving young people

- Do not be tokenistic. Involving and consulting with young people means providing appropriate services and involving the end user in developing those services. It is also about giving young people a real voice and an opportunity to develop skills and knowledge.

- Ask young people's opinions in such a way that allows them to express them freely and not give the answers that they feel adults or professionals want to hear. Ask open questions, allow young people to explore ideas and do not restrict their options.

- Do not raise false expectations. Ensure that young people understand what they can and cannot influence, and what will happen to their suggestions; and that they get feedback about the process and outcomes.

- Continue to involve young people throughout the planning, delivery and assessment of services.

- It is not necessary to work with the same young people throughout the life of a project; some will inevitably move on. It is important, therefore, to create opportunities for involvement that can cope with what may be a changing group of people.

- Talk to the youth service about existing mechanisms for consulting with and involving young people.

- Ensure young people are involved in an appropriate way. Do not automatically use the same consultation methods that work with other groups.

- Look at the organisational culture of a project and assess what needs to happen for young people's views to be received positively. Do staff have the skills required? Is this work valued sufficiently to allow staff to take the time required to perform it properly?

- Involving young people is about giving information as well as taking it. In order to make a meaningful contribution young people need to be given specific opportunities to ask for the information they need.

- Young people who are involved in consultation and other forms of involvement are giving their time. Consideration should be given to whether they should be paid or remunerated in some other way.

The Nucleus, Derry City: A project staffed and managed by young people

The Nucleus provides a range of services including a coffee bar, entertainment, an accredited peer education course, a health counselling service and a rights advice service. The centre and services are managed and staffed by young people, employing four part-time and five full-time workers, plus 12 peer educators. The youth management committee works in coordination with an advisory panel of professionals.

The service developed from work carried out by the Family Planning Service and two health workers. Young people then undertook three months of research to establish the kind of services needed in the Derry City Council area. The Nucleus is supported by most community groups in the city and can use their expertise when required. This enables them to help young people deal with a range of issues, such as drugs, alcohol, homelessness and sexual abuse.

The Plymouth foyer scheme: Consultation with young people through focus groups and interviews where young people were provided with information in advance and remunerated

When Devon and Cornwall Housing Association took over the development of the Plymouth foyer scheme, they commissioned an investigation from the University of Plymouth to establish the views of young people on its layout, operation and organisation. Young people were recruited through local agencies and paid for their involvement in focus groups and group and individual interviews. Participants were encouraged to add their own items for discussion. The group interviews allowed interaction between individuals and generated debate. The individual interviews allowed young people to express views that they felt unable to raise in the group, and gave quieter people a chance to voice their opinion.

→

Participants were provided with information about foyers in advance so that they could contribute properly. Confidentiality was maintained throughout; participants were told that all data would be used for analysis purposes only and that they could withdraw at any point.

The findings of the study confirmed the need for a foyer in Plymouth, but indicated that it needed a new design brief.

Ways of involving young people

Young people can be involved in a whole range of activities, such as assessing need; developing strategies and services; recruiting and training staff; monitoring and evaluation; developing policies and procedures; campaigning work; publicity; fundraising; and peer education. Ways of involving young people include:

- **Young people's forums:** These may focus specifically on housing or have a broader remit. These forums can establish two-way communication with professional forums.

- **Focus groups:** Specific groups of young people brought together to discuss particular issues and establish their opinions.

- **Interviews operating within a flexible agenda:** These can be individual or group interviews (see chapter 3 for more information).

- **Questionnaires and surveys:** Written or verbal. A written questionnaire is often followed up with a more in-depth face to face interview.

- **Conferences:** These can be a good way for young people to highlight their concerns, especially if they are involved in organising them. Young people can also be involved in organising a conference, increasing their control over a project.

- **Residential events:** These work best as part of a longer-term involvement.

- **Participatory appraisals:** Also known as community appraisals or community assessments. Local communities or groups carry out research, using the findings to develop action plans.

- **Tenants' and residents' associations:** Young people may wish to be involved in established associations or to set up a youth association with links with a tenants' association. Residents' meetings may be more appropriate for young people in short stay accommodation.

- **Suggestion boxes:** A straightforward and anonymous way to obtain individual comments.

Community Council for Berkshire: A project that has supported the use of participatory appraisals with young people

The Community Council for Berkshire (CCB) is an independent local development agency and registered charity whose aim is to help Berkshire residents, particularly those who are disadvantaged, to achieve a high quality of life through strengthening voluntary action and sustaining communities.

In 1997, the CCB facilitated a community appraisal in the Great Hollands area of Bracknell. Great Hollands is an area with a young population profile and was selected because of its existing networks and the problems it faced. Over 250 people were involved in assessing their community and helping to put together an action plan to tackle some of the issues of most concern. Oxfam's UK anti-poverty unit funded a participatory appraisal consultant to assist with the work and train members of the local community to carry out the appraisal.

Over 100 young people aged 13-17 were involved in the community assessment. (Problems encountered in reaching those aged over 17 would need to be addressed in similar projects in future.) Their concerns included the general problems of growing up; feeling misunderstood, often stereotyped and treated badly by others in the community; and difficulties over the lack of late-night public transport and the cost of travel.

The associated action plan included developing a schools project to bring old and young people together; a meeting between young people and the police to discuss concerns such as stereotyping; and the development of a youth club to offer support and guidance.

☐ Conclusion and checklist

Ensuring that a strategy combines being positive and imaginative with being realistic and achievable is not an easy task. It requires commitment to the aim of improving young people's housing options from a wide range of organisations with differing priorities and cultures. It also requires persistence, patience and trust — and, crucially, the involvement of young people themselves.

In developing a strategic approach to young people's housing it is important to:

- Adopt a joint working approach and choose the appropriate partners carefully.

- Be clear about the aims and principles that underpin the strategy.

- Ensure the strategy is a realistic and achievable plan that addresses the four stages of audit and research, strategy, implementation and development, and monitoring and evaluation.

- Ensure that the strategic plan links in with other key strategies where appropriate.

- Establish a multi-agency forum to assist in delivering the strategy.

- Involve young people throughout the strategic process.

CHAPTER 3

Needs Assessment

☐ Introduction

A proper assessment of what young people actually need is essential to establish what housing and other services should be provided. Needs assessment is the first crucial step in the strategic process, and must be carried out in a thorough, systematic and meaningful way. A proper needs assessment will enable the development of a strategy that is targeted appropriately, gains commitment from partner agencies, and results in services that improve young people's housing options.

This chapter addresses needs assessment. It looks at housing needs and the broader issue of service needs, concentrating on the factors that are specific to young people.

☐ Defining needs assessment

Each local authority housing department is required to carry out an assessment of housing need in its area. Section 8 of the Housing Act 1985 states that "Every local housing authority shall consider housing conditions in their district and the needs of the district with respect to the provision of further housing accommodation." Section 1 of the Housing (Scotland) Act 1987 imposes the same duty, and stresses that local authorities should work in partnership with housing associations to ensure that the supply of new social housing is properly targeted to meet local housing needs. Schedule 2 of the Children Act 1989 and schedule 2 of the Children (Northern Ireland) Order 1995 both state that "Every local authority shall take reasonable steps to identify the extent to which there are children in need in their area."

Needs assessment is not simply a numbers game, however. The difference between a crude measure of the number of bedspaces and the number of people seeking accommodation, for example, will do little to inform decisions about gaps in provision. Needs assessment should also establish the level of need for a range of services, such as advice and employment training provision. In order to do this, the process should take account of young people's needs; examine why some services are under-used and some oversubscribed; and explore the relationships between information, access and the suitability of provision (see chapter 4). It is important to bear in mind, too, that young people are at a transitional stage in their lives, so their needs may change rapidly. Strategies that seek to improve their housing options need to be wide-ranging and imaginative.

The level of need can be measured using quantitative data or qualitative research. Both are necessary to provide a full picture. Quantitative data provides a summary of the current position; qualitative research explores experiences, explanations and aspirations.

A successful needs assessment demands a multi-agency approach (see chapter 2). Different agencies may have widely differing views about the level of need in the area. Local authorities need to be aware that young people are often reluctant to approach statutory bodies and may be more inclined to use voluntary agencies or more informal settings such as youth clubs.

☐ Housing needs assessment

Local authority housing departments need to take into account a wide range of factors when carrying out their local housing needs assessment (see Box 3a on page 18). This section gives an overview of general needs assessment models providing a context for specific work on young people's needs.

There are four main models for establishing housing need (Whitehead and Kleinman, 1992).

- **Crude household/dwelling balance figure:** This is simply a measure of the number of households minus the number of dwellings and takes no account of standards, location or affordability.
- **Net stock measures:** This approach takes projected household growth and makes assumptions about the level of owner occupation, giving a residual demand for rented housing which includes a backlog of need. A modified version of the net stock model was used by Holmans in providing evidence to the Select Committee Inquiry into Housing Need (HMSO 1996).

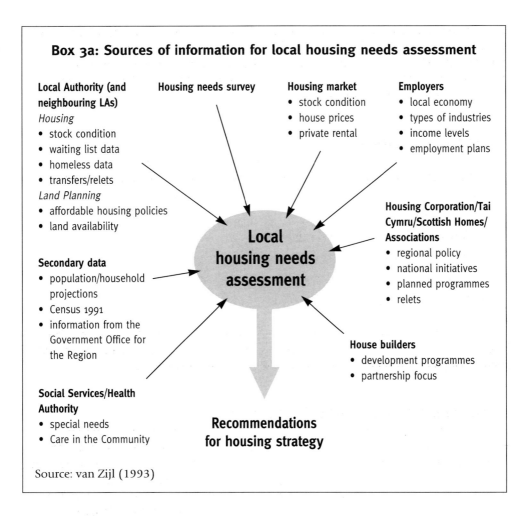

Box 3a: Sources of information for local housing needs assessment

Local Authority (and neighbouring LAs)
Housing
- stock condition
- waiting list data
- homeless data
- transfers/relets

Land Planning
- affordable housing policies
- land availability

Secondary data
- population/household projections
- Census 1991
- information from the Government Office for the Region

Social Services/Health Authority
- special needs
- Care in the Community

Housing needs survey

Housing market
- stock condition
- house prices
- private rental

Employers
- local economy
- types of industries
- income levels
- employment plans

Housing Corporation/Tai Cymru/Scottish Homes/ Associations
- regional policy
- national initiatives
- planned programmes
- relets

House builders
- development programmes
- partnership focus

Local housing needs assessment

Recommendations for housing strategy

Source: van Zijl (1993)

- **Affordability measures:** This establishes what percentage of the population can afford to become owner occupiers, leaving a residual requirement for social housing. This model was used by Bramley's study for the Association of District Councils in 1989.

- **Gross flows model:** This is a dynamic model looking at movements within the housing system and between tenures. It was used by Holmans for the 1977 Housing Policy Review and repeated in 1994 by Kleinman, Morrison and Whitehead.

Assessing the need for supported housing

The need for supported housing should be assessed in conjunction with social services departments, health authorities, the probation service, the special needs housing register and others. The **Pathways Model** was developed by Watson and Harker (1993) specifically for establishing the level of need for supported housing and draws on the gross flows model described above. For further guidance on local housing needs assessment, refer to van Zijl (1993) — see References and further reading.

☐ Service needs assessment

In addition to establishing the level of housing need in an area, it is also crucial to establish the need for associated services. These include:

- Support services
- Advice and information services
- Preparation for leaving home/education work
- Employment training services
- Rent deposit and other affordability schemes

Qualitative methods are usually the most appropriate for this type of assessment. These include participatory appraisals (see chapter 2), questionnaires, interviews, focus groups and research projects (see below for further discussion).

☐ Assessing young people's needs

It is essential to consult young people during the needs assessment process to ensure that their needs are accurately reflected in the resulting strategy document and that the document is recognised by all involved as a true picture of the situation. It is also important to try to assess young people *preferences* as well as crude needs, not least so that policy is tailored towards what they actually require rather than what professionals think is appropriate.

There are numerous sources of information and ways of doing this. This section focuses on five:

- People presenting themselves as homeless (homeless presentations)
- Snapshot surveys
- Questionnaires and interviews
- Focus groups
- Research projects

A summary table of advantages and disadvantages of each of these approaches can be found in Box 3b (page 24).

People presenting themselves as homeless

The number of homeless presentations is a basic piece of information that should inform the assessment (see Box 3a). It is clearly a crucial indicator of the lack of appropriate accommodation in the area. However, it must not be taken as representing a definitive number of young people in need of accommodation.

Firstly, it is only intended to measure those in a crisis situation who need accommodation immediately. In fact, it is unlikely even to do this. Young people are often wary about approaching statutory bodies and are more likely to seek assistance from voluntary agencies, through more informal channels or from an agency that deals specifically with young people. They may also feel that the local authority will not be able to assist them, so that some never make an application.

There are similar problems with using social services' figures of the number of young people who have requested an assessment under the Children Act — with the added complication that many social services departments do not keep records of who has approached them and what the outcome was.

Snapshot surveys

Snapshot surveys provide a picture of need at a given point in time. It is important to set clear objectives, which will determine the questions. It may be appropriate to run a pilot survey to ensure that the questions are unambiguously targeted to secure the necessary information.

It is also necessary to determine the period covered by the snapshot. It must last long enough to allow a representative picture to emerge, and prevent unusual and infrequent events from skewing the results. At the same time, it must not be so long that agencies are unwilling to be involved or the process becomes unwieldy. It is crucial to ensure that all the relevant agencies are involved, and are consulted throughout the process.

The survey form should be kept short, with clear instructions and terminology, since most staff will be completing it on top of an already busy workload. Snapshot surveys can be time-consuming and need to be carefully planned, with sufficient time for analysis built into the process.

It is important to avoid double counting. A relatively fail-safe way to do this is by using the young person's initials and date of birth as a unique identifier. This identifier also enables young people to remain anonymous while remaining part of the survey. (See chapter 10.)

In assessing the outcome of snapshot surveys, it is important to consider an overview rather than each individual agency's performance. For example, some agencies may consider referral to another agency a successful outcome; clearly this can produce a false picture. In the case study in Rugby detailed below,

50 individuals visited more than one agency; some visited as many as five agencies without an appropriate housing outcome being achieved. Following through the procedures and interactions provides the full picture.

Rugby: A snapshot survey with clear instructions and working definitions

During August-October 1996, Centrepoint Warwickshire coordinated a monitoring exercise in Rugby, commissioned by the local inter-agency forum. All relevant agencies were sent a standard monitoring form on which to collect basic personal details: the young person's current housing situation and reasons for it; other agencies with which they had contact; any additional needs; and the outcome of contact with that agency. The attached 'Notes on completion' outlined the working definition of homelessness to be used as well as explaining the aims of the exercise. The results were distributed in both tabular and summary form.

A particular kind of snapshot survey is provided by counts of the number of people sleeping rough. Young people are over-represented among rough-sleepers, so any assessment of need in an area should include some estimate of those without a roof of any sort over their heads.

Questionnaires and interviews

Questionnaires and interviews can provide a more comprehensive picture of young people's experiences. Questionnaires can be used as a precursor to more in-depth interviews, or either approach can be used on its own. If follow-up interviews are used, there must be a mechanism for tracking down individuals after the questionnaire stage. This may be difficult to achieve in large towns and cities.

As with snapshot surveys, it is important to involve a wide range of agencies throughout the process, including in the design of the questionnaire. Training should be given to staff who complete the questionnaires with homeless young people. It is important to ensure that young people do not complete the questionnaires more than once. Agencies must also explain to young people why they are being asked to complete the questionnaire and the impact it is likely to have on their situation.

Interviews do not have to be questionnaire-based, but can be more open-ended while still following a framework. The best approach will depend on the information required, which in turn depends on the objectives of the exercise. Interviews must be undertaken by someone with the training and experience both to carry out the interviews and analyse the results.

Rhondda Cynon Taff: A survey involving questionnaires, follow-up interviews and a street count which resulted in a change to the local authority allocation system

Rhondda Cynon Taff housing department commissioned the University of Glamorgan to carry out a survey of single people's housing needs during January-April 1997. The survey, which lasted two weeks, involved questionnaires administered by a wide range of agencies. The questionnaire was designed by representatives from these agencies, drawing on similar ones already in use in other parts of the country. It was followed up by in-depth interviews. The interviews were considered crucial as they enabled the authority to look at the processes underlying an individual's circumstances. The survey also involved a night-time street count. As a result of this survey, the local authority revised its points system for allocating permanent housing, making it more advantageous for single people, and began to award points for rough sleeping.

Focus groups

Focus groups concentrate on the interviewees' perspective. The discussion focuses on the views of the young people participating while operating within a flexible agenda. The emphasis and weight of each topic is dictated to a great extent by the young people themselves and not the researcher. Young people should also be encouraged to set their own agenda. If the topics brought by the researcher do not reflect what is important to them, then they should be encouraged to discuss what they feel is more important. (See also chapter 2.)

Focus groups can be applied to a wide range of purposes, including funding applications. They can facilitate innovative, wide-ranging solutions as well as an assessment of need. The nature of focus groups allows young people to 'take ownership' of the issues and increase their understanding of the situation, thereby developing more realistic expectations. This methodology is time consuming, however, and requires experienced staff.

Kirklees Metropolitan Council: Use of focus groups to assist in developing a Single Regeneration Budget funding bid

Kirklees housing services department worked with focus groups of young people, particularly the Lowerhouses Youth Build Access Project, in preparing a Single Regeneration Budget bid.

→

Contact with young people was already well advanced through the work of a very active team of community development officers from both the community development services and housing services departments.

Evidence from young people at Lowerhouses supported the bid. A number of young people involved in the SRB theme groups became involved in the project development groups, which were working up specific bids for submission. Young people also attended a residential weekend with others representing other bids. Their level of involvement gave them a greater appreciation of the decisions taken. One said, "My project didn't get through but because I've been involved I understand why — what matters is that the rest of the bid is successful."

Research projects

A dedicated research project addressing the needs of young people in an area can provide a strong foundation for a strategy. This sort of project can prove expensive, however, and is most appropriately supported by a range of agencies (see chapter 2). A local university or an independent body may be well placed to carry out the research.

A project of this type should use a combination of primary and secondary sources. Much of the information may already be available, but held by a number of different organisations and individuals. One of the key aims, therefore, should be to draw together all relevant existing information. Additional primary research, such as a snapshot survey, is also extremely valuable, particularly in areas where there may be a shortage of existing statistics available. Underpinning it all, the views of young people should be obtained to ensure that the exercise gives a representative and credible picture. The resulting document should build in strategic planning and development.

Centrepoint Devon: A detailed research project into needs and resources resulting in a strategic plan

Centrepoint Devon is a three year project funded by the Rural Development Commission, the Northbrook Community Trust, the William Sutton Trust and others. The first six months involved detailed research into housing needs and resources in the area. This was followed by two and a half years assisting partner agencies in developing services and policies in line with the research report's strategic recommendations.

→

The action research involved detailed consultation with local agencies through semi-structured interviews seeking facts, opinions and anecdotes. There were set targets for the range of people to be consulted, with additional contacts as the research progressed. The initial intention was to draw solely on secondary research, but the lack of data in certain parts of the county made it necessary to carry out a snapshot survey of need. Young people were also consulted, including those using youth clubs and drop-in centres as well as those seeking immediate assistance.

Box 3b: Methods of assessing young people's needs: advantages and disadvantages

	Advantages	Disadvantages
Homeless presentations	Key indicator of need Easy to collate	Incomplete picture Young people often reluctant to approach statutory bodies
Snapshot surveys	Time-limited exercise Gives a picture across a range of agencies	Coordination of agencies Provides little information on processes or appropriate solutions
Questionnaires and interviews	Provides information on reasons, processes and solutions	Time consuming Small sample
Focus groups	Gain young people's perspective Can explore themes, ideas and solutions	Time consuming Organisational culture
Research projects	Can use a wide range of sources of information Consultation with wide range of organisations and young people	Time consuming Resource intensive

☐ Conclusion and checklist

Needs assessment is the first stage of the strategic process and, combined with an audit of existing resources, will make it possible to draw up a strategy for developing services. Housing needs must be central to this assessment, but it must also assess the need for associated services. The methodology must be appropriate to the needs of young people and provide a comprehensive picture.

In carrying out a needs assessment it is important to:

- Take into account the requirements placed on statutory bodies to carry out needs assessment and integrate the resulting information into a specific needs assessment for young people.
- Ensure that the assessment addresses interactions, exploring why some services are utilised and others are not (see chapter 4).
- Use both qualitative and quantitative methods to provide a comprehensive picture.
- Involve a multi-agency approach to ensure a full picture of the situation.
- Be mindful of the wide range of information sources and include supported housing.
- Ensure that a service needs assessment is also undertaken.
- Ensure that the methodologies chosen are appropriate for assessing young people's needs, and that sufficient resources are available.

CHAPTER 4

Audit of Resources

☐ Introduction

Carrying out an audit of resources will lead to a greater understanding of current property, services, finance and organisational arrangements, and assist in identifying the potential for building on and adding to existing resources. It should also take account of provision that is planned or in development. To complete this process successfully it is essential to adopt a multi-agency approach (see chapter 2). Different agencies will be aware of different services for young people, and will have their own views on how effective these services are.

This chapter looks at auditing accommodation and other services; ways of using that information; making the best use of existing provision; and financial and organisational resources.

☐ Audit of provision

An audit of existing provision in an area must go beyond accommodation to consider associated services. It must look across all sectors — public, private and voluntary — to provide a comprehensive picture. It must also be updated regularly, since a one-off audit will soon become out of date.

Audit of accommodation

An audit of accommodation can be broken down in a number of ways, according to tenure, length of stay or level of support provision. It should provide significantly more information than a crude count of bedspaces. A range of information can be collected (see Box 4a).

It may also be appropriate to gather qualitative information on issues such as:

- Why is certain accommodation underused?
- Why is certain accommodation oversubscribed?
- Why does the popularity of certain provision go through phases?

In answering these questions it will be necessary to look at:

- Location
- Transport
- Publicity
- Rules and regulations
- Are projects age-specific or are young people living with older people?
- What personal relationships exist between individuals and groups of young people?
- What reputation do different projects have?

Box 4a: Audit of accommodation

In carrying out an audit of accommodation it is important to consider a wide range of factors:

- Stock condition: "A knowledge of the condition of the local housing stock is clearly fundamental to an authority in developing and pursuing its housing strategy." (Department of Environment, 1995)
- Standards, including the private rented sector
- The target group and excluded categories
- Length of stay
- Equal opportunities
- Staff training
- Rent levels and other charges: compare to maximum benefit levels
- Void levels
- Move-on arrangements
- Support offered
- Referral procedures
- Residential rights

Audit of services

It is important to establish what related services exist in an area. An audit of services should include the following:

- Advice and information services
- Support services
- Employment training services
- Preparation for leaving home/education work

Directory of local provision

An audit of provision will contribute to the strategic planning process, but it can also provide the raw data for a directory of local provision. A directory providing comprehensive information in an accessible format can be extremely valuable to advice services and for young people directly. This will also need to be regularly updated.

Vacant bedspace information service

It is also possible to develop a service that provides up to data information on vacant bedspaces. This is most appropriate for direct-access and short or medium-stay projects.

This sort of information service can be provided in a number of ways, depending on the available resources. One agency may take responsibility for collating the information, possibly on a database, with regular updates from other agencies. If an agency then requires information on current vacancies, they simply telephone the coordinating agency. This method does not require access to information technology to participate. All that is required is a telephone. But if participating agencies have access to the Internet, a database can be set up which all agencies can access. They would only be able to amend information relating to their own agency, but would be able to view information about all vacancies.

Information from a vacant bedspace information service can be fed into an evaluation of the local situation (see chapter 10).

Bolton Accommodation Guide and Bed Line

The *Bolton Accommodation Guide* provides a comprehensive list of temporary and supported housing options. The guide was developed by Bolton Inter-Agency Forum and Bolton Resettlement and Support Workers Forum, and is maintained by the special needs officer in the housing department.

→

The Bolton Bed Line is a central 'clearing house' for receiving and distributing information about vacancies in temporary accommodation, removing the need for other agencies to spend time ringing around. Accommodation providers fax up-to-date details of vacancies to Bed Line, which faxes out details to participating agencies on Monday and Thursday mornings.

Hostels Online Project

Centrepoint's Berwick Street hostel is part of a pilot project developed by Resource Information Services and funded by the DETR. The project currently involves six direct-access hostels, but is likely to be extended, including to longer-stay projects. The service provides access to the Internet to enable project workers to update and access information about hostel vacancies. Resource Information Services also provides a London-wide hostel directory on disk. Although this is not 'live', it does enable projects to search for hostels that will accept particular young people: for example, it is possible to carry out a search against various criteria, such as '17 years old', 'refugee' and 'female'.

Making the best use of existing provision

The best possible use of existing social housing stock should be considered as part of a strategic approach, as outlined by the Housing Corporation in relation to Approved Development Programme investment (see Box 4b). In particular, there is, rightly, an increasing demand for empty properties to be brought back into use. Any audit of resources should look closely at what might be done to improve the use of existing housing.

Local authorities often find themselves with difficult-to-let units. For example, social landlords may find it useful to undertake a review of their difficult-to-let sheltered schemes and assess whether the properties are suitable for young people's housing. Sheltered accommodation is often in the form of bedsits, which are unpopular with older people but may be appropriate for many young people with low support needs. Move-on arrangements must form an integral part of planning such a project.

Other types of housing should also be considered for a change of use when seeking to meet young people's needs. If the strategic planning process has identified the need for a foyer scheme, for example, it may be appropriate to use existing miscellaneous properties for a dispersed foyer. This may be particularly appropriate bearing in mind that it is rarely appropriate to locate a large number of young people in one area. If this does happen it must be carefully planned and managed. An on-site manager or caretaker may be most appropriate.

It should be remembered, too, that the vast majority of empty property is in the private sector. Initiatives with private owners, such as schemes to utilise flats above shops, can make a major contribution to local provision.

Grenfell Housing Association: An association providing short term accommodation to young people using former sheltered accommodation for older people

The Gables is a short-term shared housing scheme providing temporary accommodation for single people aged 18-30. It was formerly a London Borough of Merton sheltered scheme for older people. The property contains 17 fully-furnished bedsits, including one for a 'responsible tenant' who has some caretaking duties. There are six shared bathrooms and a communal lounge. Young people can stay for up to one year, and Grenfell has negotiated three general needs vacancies each year as move-on accommodation.

Calgarth Road, Knowsley: Use of a specific area with a resident manager for young people's housing

Calgarth Road contains 52 mainly one-bed units set around a central green. When Knowsley's Young Person's Accommodation Scheme was started in 1995, over half the properties were vacant. Its reputation had become so bad that there was a complete absence of demand for the accommodation and many of the remaining tenants were requesting transfers. Knowsley housing department decided to turn the area into a project specifically for young people. The key to making the project work was the appointment of a resident manager to liaise with outside agencies and council departments, and to supervise, manage and caretake the scheme. The resident manager interviews all prospective tenants and explains the code of conduct, which is crucial to the project's success. Tenants pay an extra £10 per week for the manager's services.

Box 4b: Local housing strategies — a frame of reference for Approved Development Programme investment in England

What is the shape, scale, location etc. of anticipated future need for social and other housing?
- client groups?
- need for support?
- relationship with wider issues, e.g. local economy, transport, health, recreation?
- who has contributed to the assessment?
- how robust are the figures?

What is the existing supply of housing in relation to these needs (all tenures)?
- including developments already under way

What is the nature and scale of future demand/supply mismatch?
- in each locality?
- overall numbers?
- condition of existing stock?
- suitability of existing stock?

Government and Corporation strategies and priorities e.g.
- private finance and transfers
- community care
- regeneration
- empty properties
- rural village housing
- home ownership
- housing for older people
- supported housing
- black and ethnic minority housing
- tenant participation

What can be done to get best use out of the existing stock (all tenures) to meet the future need?
- nominations/referrals?
- move-on?
- repairs?
- sales or transfers of existing social housing?
- refurbishments?
- remodelling?
- demolitions (with or without replacement)?
- aids/adaptations?
- change of client group?
- floating support?
- refocusing existing supported housing management grant (SHMG)?
- SHMG for existing general needs dwellings?
- new technology?
- leasing?
- temporary social housing?
- Tenants Incentive Scheme?
- Do-It-Yourself Shared Ownership?
- Cash Incentive Scheme?

Investment possibilities:
- Approved Development Programme?
- Housing Investment Programme?
- private finance?
- Private Finance Initiative?
- Registered social landlords' own resources?
- Estates Renewal Challenge Fund?
- Single Regeneration Budget?

What are the priority gaps between existing provision and future needs meriting Approved Development Programme investment?
- what are the priority needs (30-60 year timeframe)?
- how location-specific are they?
  (Cost-benefit consideration of alternative locations, taking account of the facilities and services needed by the prospective clients)
- what Scheme Development Standards-Plus or Housing Plus spin-offs or bolt-ons should we be looking for?
- who is going to provide the non-housing elements needed to ensure a sustainable community?

Source: Housing Corporation

- what are the relevant parameters for competition?
- how best to organise competition?

☐ Financial resources

Securing funding

A needs assessment and audit of provision will identify the areas that require additional funds, and provide information for a well-argued case to secure them. Detailed information about sources of funding is not within the scope of this guide. See Box 4c, however, for a checklist of sources of funding.

Box 4c: Checklist of sources of funding

- Single Regeneration Budget/Urban Programme
- European funding
- Housing Corporation/Tai Cymru/Scottish Homes/Northern Ireland Housing Executive — capital and revenue
- The National Lottery
- English Partnerships
- Local authority grants to voluntary organisations
- Joint finance
- Mental Illness Specific Grant
- Drug Specific Grant
- Rough Sleepers Initiative
- Local authority capital programme and capital receipts
- Rural Development Commission
- Section 180 funding, Housing Act 1996
- Probation Accommodation Grant Scheme
- Charitable trusts, including the Housing Associations Charitable Trust and the Scottish Housing Associations Charitable Trust
- Housing benefit
- Social services payments under the Children Act
- Welsh Capital Challenge
- Strategic Development Scheme — Welsh Office
- Youth service
- Training and Enterprise Councils and Local Enterprise Companies
- Employment Service
- Renovation grants to private landlords

The London Borough of Croydon housing department employs a range of funding options for accommodating young people

Croydon Council funds a local voluntary organisation to provide a lodgings scheme. The scheme aims to find suitable householders with spare rooms and then interview and place homeless young people. This is followed up with some support to help maintain the placement, such as benefits assistance and mediation. The scheme has been awarded both DETR and charitable funding to extend the service.

Supported Housing Management Grant is used for a floating support scheme for care leavers nominated by social services and rehoused in housing association tenancies.

The council is exploring the use of local authority Social Housing Grant for developing a foyer scheme. The project will be given a high priority in the Housing Investment Programme but will depend on resources. Other sources of funding are being investigated to cover revenue costs. It is anticipated that this will be integrated into New Deal initiatives.

A large hostel for 17 to 25-year-olds has recently been extensively refurbished using Social Housing Grant. Croydon has agreed to fund extra unanticipated costs involved in the development using capital receipts.

Use of capital expenditure

The release of capital receipts by the new Labour government in 1997 focused attention on the use of capital expenditure. Decisions over its use and bids for funding should be made in line with the priorities identified during the strategic planning process, making sure that young people's needs are taken into account.

Some authorities may not have sufficient funding for a new supported housing project each year. It may be desirable, then, to come together with other authorities in the area, pool all supported housing funding and allocate it according to jointly agreed priorities. This approach depends on good joint working and cooperation, and good quality information about the level of need. One example where this sort of joint approach has been used for some years now involves the five district housing departments in Warwickshire, which have each top-sliced seven per cent of their share of the Approved Development Programme for special needs projects. The allocations are then pooled to fund one or more schemes that satisfy the criteria of the local special needs housing consortium.

Oxford City Council: A strategic process for identifying supported housing priorities

Oxford City Council has developed a housing (strategy for single people) working party, which meets quarterly. The group is made up of councillors and representatives from the housing department, social services, the health authority and trusts, the probation service, the voluntary sector and the housing association forum. The group identifies key objectives for the year, which currently include:

- reviewing existing services and developing comprehensive day and residential services for young people;
- providing 25 per cent of accommodation for single people within any new development and rehabilitation programmes; and
- aiming to provide adequate move-on accommodation from new and existing schemes.

The working party also has a key role in selecting special needs housing projects for specific council properties.

☐ Organisational resources

An audit of resources needs to include organisational resources. Information on existing policies and strategies should be taken into account when developing work on young people's housing needs. It may become apparent that it is not necessary to set up a new strategy group. This exercise will also highlight which other strategies a youth strategy should be feeding into.

☐ Conclusion and checklist

An assessment of needs and resources is the essential first stage of the strategic planning process. The next stage is to identify the need for new services, and how and by whom they might be developed. Once these options have been identified they need to be prioritised. All new work should fit into this process; otherwise it will produce unnecessary repetition and use up valuable resources.

An audit of resources should:

- Take a multi-agency approach and look at accommodation, services and financial and organisational resources.
- Take account of planned services and those in development, as well as those already in use.
- Decide what information about accommodation to collect, and consider collecting information that provides information on why provision is or is not used.
- Consider other uses for the information collected to inform the strategic process, such as a directory of local provision and a vacant bedspace information service.
- Ensure best use is being made of existing provision.
- Involve different agencies working together to ensure maximum access to funding.
- Develop a clear strategy for capital investment. Consider pooling resources with neighbouring areas if funding levels are low.
- Remember to take account of organisational resources such as strategies and policies.

CHAPTER 5

Joint Working using the Housing and Children's Legislation

☐ Introduction

Although housing and social services departments have always been allowed to work together, recent children's legislation has placed a corporate responsibility on social services authorities towards young people in housing need. As a result, many authorities have significantly developed their work in this area.

This chapter details the relevant sections of the Children Act 1989, Children (Scotland) Act 1995, Children (Northern Ireland) Order 1995, Housing Act 1996, Housing (Scotland) Act 1987 and Housing (Northern Ireland) Order 1988. It discusses joint approaches to working with the legislation, including joint planning; procedures and protocols; assessments and definitions; the use of advocacy services; and the housing register and allocations.

☐ The legislation

The key sections of the legislation that relate to young people in housing need are detailed below. The legislation and related guidance must be referred to for full details.

The DETR is due to publish a revised Code of Guidance on Parts VI and VII of the Housing Act 1996 during 1998. Since it is expected to contain additional references to single homeless people and possibly homeless young people, this chapter should be read with reference to any such revisions.

Box 5a: Children Act 1989, implemented in England and Wales on 14 October 1991

Section 17(10) A 'child in need' is defined as:

(a) those unlikely to achieve or maintain, or have the opportunity of achieving or maintaining, a reasonable standard of health or development without the provision of services;

(b) those whose health or development is likely to be significantly impaired, or further impaired, without the provision of such services;

(c) those who are disabled.

Section 20(3) Every social services authority has a duty to provide accommodation for any 'child in need' who has reached the age of 16, and whose welfare is likely to be 'seriously prejudiced' without accommodation.

Section 20 (6) The authority has a duty to ascertain the child's wishes and give due consideration to them.

Section 24(1) The authority has a duty to advise, assist and befriend a child who is being looked after with a view to promoting their welfare when they cease to be looked after.

Section 24(2) Social services authorities have a duty to advise, assist and befriend a young person who has been looked after by the authority after they reached the age of 16. This applies until they reach the age of 21.

Section 27(1) Social services authorities have a power to request the help of other authorities, including the local housing authority, to enable them to comply with their duties to provide accommodation.

Section 27(2) It is, then, a duty of the other authority to assist so far as this would be compatible with that authority's own statutory duties and does not unduly prejudice the discharge of any of their functions.

Box 5b: Children (Scotland) Act 1995, Part II, implemented April 1997

Section 93 (4) A 'child in need' is defined as:

(a) those unlikely to achieve or maintain, or have the opportunity of achieving or maintaining, a reasonable standard of health or development without the provision of services by a local authority;

(b) those whose health or development is likely to be significantly impaired, or further impaired, without the provision of such services;

(c) those who are disabled;

(d) those who are adversely affected by the disability of another member of their family.

Section 25(2) A local authority has the power to provide accommodation for any child in its area aged 16 or 17 if they consider that to do so would safeguard or promote their welfare.

Section 25(3) A local authority has the power to provide accommodation to anyone aged 18-20 in its area if they consider that to do so would safeguard or promote their welfare.

Section 17(1) Local authorities have the duty to safeguard and promote the welfare of 16 and 17-year-olds when they are 'looked after'.

Section 17(2) Local authorities have the duty to prepare young people for leaving care.

Section 17(3) Local authorities are required to ascertain so far as is practically possible the views of the child before making a decision with respect to a child whom they are looking after or proposing to look after.

Section 29(1) Local authorities have the duty to provide after-care support for young people looked after at school-leaving age or later until they reach the age of 19 unless satisfied that their welfare does not require such support.

Section 29(2) Local authorities have the power to provide after-care support for young people looked after at school-leaving age or later until they reach the age of 19 where the young person makes a request for such support.

Section 25(5) Local authorities must have regard to the views of the child in making any decision to provide them with advice and assistance or with accommodation.

Box 5c: Children (Northern Ireland) Order 1995, implemented on 4 November 1996

Article 17 A 'child in need' is defined as:

  (a) those unlikely to achieve or maintain, or have the opportunity of achieving or maintaining, a reasonable standard of health or development without the provision of services;

  (b) those whose health or development is likely to be significantly impaired, or further impaired, without the provision of such services;

  (c) those who are disabled.

Article 21(3) Local authorities have the duty to provide accommodation for any child in need who has reached the age of 16 and whose welfare is likely to be seriously prejudiced without accommodation.

Article 21(5) Local authorities have the power to provide accommodation until the child reaches 21 if it is thought this would safeguard or promote their welfare.

Article 21(6) The local authority has a duty to ascertain the child's wishes and give due consideration to them.

Article 35 (1) The local authority has a duty to advise, assist and befriend a child who is being 'looked after' with a view to promoting their welfare when they cease to be looked after.

Article 35 (2) Local authorities have a duty to advise, assist and befriend a young person, who has been looked after by the authority after they have reached the age of 16 until they reach the age of 21.

Box 5d: Housing Act 1996 Part VII, implemented 20 January 1997

Section 184 If the local authority has reason to believe that a person is homeless or threatened with homelessness they have a duty to make enquiries.

Section 185 A person is not eligible for assistance if they are a person from abroad who is ineligible for housing assistance, or they are subject to immigration control (unless they come within a number of exempt categories). (In such cases local authorities should utilise the Children Act 1989 or National Assistance Act 1948.)

Section 175 A person is homeless if they have no accommodation available in the UK or elsewhere, or if they cannot secure entry to it, or it is not reasonable for them to occupy it for reasons such as domestic violence (see section 177).

Section 189 A person is in priority need if they or their partner are pregnant; have dependent children; are vulnerable due to old age, mental illness or handicap or physical disability or other special reason; or are homeless as a result of an emergency.

Section 191 A person becomes homeless intentionally if they deliberately do or fail to do something which causes them to lose their accommodation, which was available for their occupation and which it would have been reasonable for them to continue to occupy.

Section 193 Local authorities have a duty to secure accommodation for two years if the person is found to be eligible for assistance, in priority need and unintentionally homeless. This duty is subject to section 197.

Section 197 If suitable accommodation is available in the district, and is likely to be so for two years, a local authority's duty is restricted to the provision of advice and assistance that is reasonably required to enable them to secure such accommodation (Homelessness (Suitability of Accommodation) Amendment (SI 1741/1997)).

Section 182 Local authorities must have regard to guidance given by the Secretary of State.

Box 5e: Housing (Scotland) Act 1987 Part II

Section 28 If the local authority has reason to believe that a person is homeless or threatened with homelessness they have a duty to inquire.

Section 24 A person is homeless if they have no accommodation in Scotland, England or Wales.

Section 25 A person is in priority need if they

   (a) are pregnant;

   (b) have dependent children;

   (c) are vulnerable due to old age, mental illness or handicap or physical disability or other special reason;

   (d) are a young person under 21 who was previously looked after by a local authority under the Children (Scotland) Act 1995, or were in local authority care or subject to a supervision requirement under the Social Work (Scotland) Act 1968 at school leaving age or later [The Homeless Persons (Priority Need) (Scotland) Order 1997 (SI 3049/1997)];

   (e) are homeless as a result of an emergency.

Section 26 A person becomes homeless intentionally if they deliberately do or fail to do something which causes them to lose their accommodation.

Section 31 If a person is found to be in priority need and unintentionally homeless the local authority has a duty to secure accommodation for that person.

Section 37 Local authorities shall have regard to guidance given by the Secretary of State.

Asylum and Immigration Act 1996 Section 9 (2) A person subject to immigration control shall not be eligible for accommodation or assistance under the homelessness provisions of the Housing (Scotland) Act 1987 Part II unless he is of a class specified in an Order made by the Secretary of State. (See the Code of Guidance on Homelessness for further details.)

Box 5f: Housing (Northern Ireland) Order 1988

Article 7 If the local authority has reason to believe that a person is homeless or threatened with homelessness they have a duty to inquire.

Article 3 A person is homeless if they have no accommodation in Northern Ireland.

Article 5 A person is in priority need if they

(a) are pregnant;

(b) have dependent children;

(c) are vulnerable due to old age, mental illness or handicap or physical disability or other special reason;

(d) are homeless as a result of an emergency;

(e) have been subject to violence and are at risk of violent pursuit or, if they return home, are at risk of further violence;

(f) are a young person (that is, aged 16-21) who is at risk of sexual or financial exploitation.

Article 6 A person becomes homeless intentionally if they deliberately do or fail to do something which causes them to lose their accommodation.

Article 10 If a person is found to be in priority need and unintentionally homeless the local authority has a duty to secure accommodation for that person.

Asylum and Immigration Act 1996 Section 9 (2) A person subject to immigration control shall not be eligible for accommodation or assistance under the homelessness provisions of the Housing (Northern Ireland) Order 1988 unless he is of a class specified in an Order made by the Secretary of State.

☐ Working together under the legislation

Local authority departments and voluntary agencies can work together under this legislation by:

- Joint planning
- Joint protocols and procedures
- Joint assessments
- Jointly agreed definitions of 'vulnerability' and 'in need'

These approaches are interlinked and it is difficult to separate them, so the distinctions made in the following four sections may be a little artificial. It is important, however, to recognise that each needs developing in its own right. Joint planning will not automatically lead to joint procedures; joint procedures do not necessarily involve joint assessments. Ideally, authorities should develop all levels of joint working.

All the case studies in this section are drawn from England and Wales, since the Children Act 1989 has been in place longer than the Children (Scotland) Act 1995 and Children (Northern Ireland) Order 1995. The good practice is applicable across the UK.

Joint planning

The Department of the Environment and Welsh Office Codes of Guidance on Parts VI and VII of the Housing Act 1996 (paragraph 14.14 in both cases) state: "Agreements will be most useful if they cover not only assessment, but also planning for the delivery of provision. Such agreements should be an outcome of the joint policies envisaged by the Children Act 1989 Guidance and Regulations and of the requirement on local authorities to produce Children's Service Plans on an inter-agency basis."

The Children Act 1989 (Schedule 2) requires local authority social service departments to carry out an audit of need and set up procedures to monitor the extent of need in the area, as does the Children (Scotland) Act 1995, and the Children (Northern Ireland) Order 1995 (Schedule 2).

Joint planning must ensure that children's service plans and housing strategies are compatible and refer to each other where appropriate. Other strategies must also interrelate and complement one another.

Joint protocols and procedures

The Codes of Guidance on Parts VI and VII of the Housing Act 1996 (paragraph 14.14) state: "Effective collaborative working is best facilitated by corporate policies and clear departmental procedures between social services and housing departments. Such procedures should make it clear who takes responsibility in cases where there is any room for dispute."

Likewise, the Code of Guidance on Homelessness attached to the Housing (Scotland) Act 1987 (paragraph 4.11) says: "Co-operation between housing and social work is essential. Formal liaison arrangements between housing and social work departments should be established, at local as well as central levels, and procedural protocols may be useful."

A protocol establishes the roles, responsibilities and interrelationships between organisations. (See Box 5g for the suggested scope of a protocol.) A protocol must also deal specifically with the needs of care leavers.

Box 5g: Scope of a joint protocol

- The departments' general philosophy towards homeless 16 and 17-year-olds
- Common understandings of the legislation (see 'Jointly agreed definitions' below)
- The joint assessment process and the way in which the Children Act and Housing Act are understood — i.e. the criteria by which the respective departments accept responsibility
- The provision of emergency accommodation
- The responsibilities of each agency, including individual responsibility
- What happens if a young person is not accepted under the legislation
- What assessments are to take place
- The continuing legal responsibility of the housing department in providing permanent accommodation
- The continuing legal responsibility of the social services department in providing support
- Complaints and representation
- Monitoring and review

Source: Brody, 1996

A protocol is designed to prevent departments passing young people back and forth without taking specific responsibility. Protocols can maximise the effectiveness of limited resources by ensuring that young people are dealt with only once, and at a stage before any problems become entrenched. It is far more expensive to attempt to resettle someone who has spent months or years living rough than it is to provide accommodation and support for a young person in acute housing need. Developing a protocol can also raise awareness and understanding of youth homelessness in the other departments and agencies involved.

If a protocol is to be effective it must be developed and implemented in consultation with a wide range of agencies and individuals, including voluntary organisations and frontline workers. It may be appropriate for an agency outside the local authority structure to provide longer-term support to those young people who need additional help, with financial support from the local authority.

Leicester City Council: A comprehensive joint protocol increasing understanding between departments

Leicester's joint protocol for working with homeless 16 and 17-year-olds outlines the respective and mutual responsibilities of housing and social services. It details the procedure for responding to and assessing housing and support needs, and for developing joint packages of support for identified cases.

The protocol is split into six stages:

- Initial contact
- Initial interview and investigation
- Provision of temporary accommodation
- Further investigation
- Joint assessment
- Housing and support package

Discussion of the protocol and individual cases has engendered greater understanding of the remit and pressures under which different departments operate. It has also raised awareness about youth homelessness within both housing and social services, and produced significant developments towards a one-stop service for young people.

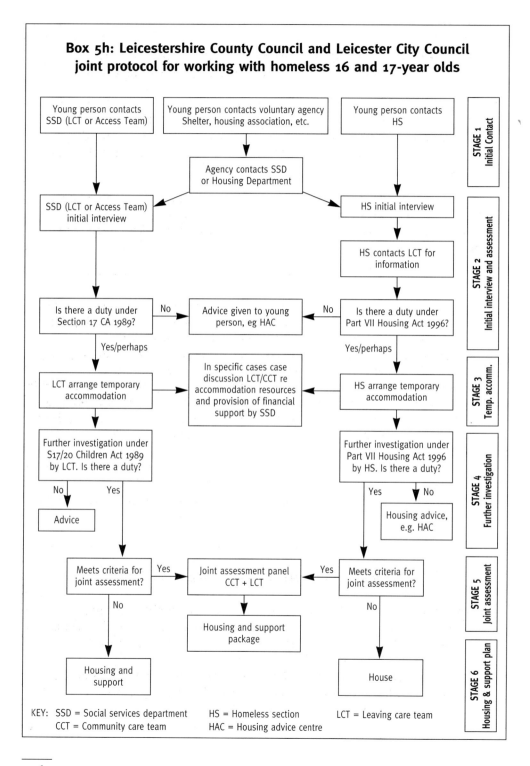

Box 5h: Leicestershire County Council and Leicester City Council joint protocol for working with homeless 16 and 17-year olds

Young person contacts SSD (LCT or Access Team)

Young person contacts voluntary agency Shelter, housing association, etc.

Young person contacts HS

STAGE 1 Initial Contact

Agency contacts SSD or Housing Department

SSD (LCT or Access Team) initial interview

HS initial interview

HS contacts LCT for information

STAGE 2 Initial interview and assessment

Is there a duty under Section 17 CA 1989? — No → Advice given to young person, eg HAC ← No — Is there a duty under Part VII Housing Act 1996?

Yes/perhaps

Yes/perhaps

LCT arrange temporary accommodation

In specific cases case discussion LCT/CCT re accommodation resources and provision of financial support by SSD

HS arrange temporary accommodation

STAGE 3 Temp. accomm.

Further investigation under S17/20 Children Act 1989 by LCT. Is there a duty?

Further investigation under Part VII Housing Act 1996 by HS. Is there a duty?

No — Yes

Yes — No

Advice

Housing advice, e.g. HAC

STAGE 4 Further investigation

Meets criteria for joint assessment? — Yes → Joint assessment panel CCT + LCT ← Yes — Meets criteria for joint assessment?

No

No

Housing and support package

STAGE 5 Joint assessment

Housing and support

House

STAGE 6 Housing & support plan

KEY: SSD = Social services department   HS = Homeless section   LCT = Leaving care team
CCT = Community care team   HAC = Housing advice centre

**Norwich Housing Services and Norfolk Social Services:
A joint protocol that clearly states young people's legal rights**

This joint protocol aims to facilitate a coordinated response to the needs of homeless young people in Norwich. It lays out the individual responsibilities of the housing and social services departments, making it clear that receiving an assessment from one department does not affect the young person's right to an assessment by the other.

The arrangements for referrals between departments are set out in detail. A standard referral form is used and the young person is given a copy. This form can also be used by advice agencies making a referral to housing or social services.

Because joint protocols have often been prompted by the Children Act, social services departments or voluntary agencies often take the lead on developing strategies for working with homeless young people. However, housing departments can, and often need to, take policy decisions with regard to young people in conjunction with social services. There is scope within the homelessness legislation for local authorities to treat young people as vulnerable, and therefore in priority need. Indeed, since 1 January 1998, young people aged under 21 who have been looked after at school leaving age or later are required to be treated as vulnerable under the Housing (Scotland) Act 1987.

If the decision is taken to treat certain young people as vulnerable and in priority need, it is important to ensure that they are allocated appropriate accommodation, provided with sufficient support, and arrangements made for moving them on into permanent independent housing.

Sheffield Young Persons' Accommodation Team

With the introduction of the Children Act 1989, Sheffield's housing department set up a young persons' accommodation team, which accepts care leavers aged 16-21 and young people 'in need' aged 16 and 17 referred from social services. The team secures appropriate accommodation and support, which may or may not be a local authority tenancy; it may be more appropriate to house the young person in a supported accommodation project for a while.

→

> The housing department officer stays in contact and once the young person is ready to move on they are awarded sufficient points to be offered independent housing. The team can also grant a tenancy and provide a support package from the leaving care team, housing department tenancy support officers, youth workers and family.

Joint assessments

While joint protocols set out how agencies should work together, joint assessment procedures either bring agencies together to carry out assessments or give responsibility to one agency to carry them out on behalf of other organisations. Again, this prevents young people being passed between departments or agencies with none taking responsibility.

If joint assessment procedures are developed, it is also necessary to establish which department has financial responsibility for the services that may be provided. This is best done through a blanket agreement — for example, splitting costs 50:50 between housing and social services departments — rather than a case-by-case arrangement.

> ### Brighton Council: A joint assessment process where costs are met jointly by housing and social services
>
> A 1991 conference led to a joint working relationship between housing and social services in Brighton. The homeless team and social services staff based at a bedsit unit carried out joint assessments to ascertain whether the young person was the responsibility of social services or the housing department, and so which department should pay for any services. In 1993, it was decided that a better service would be provided if the issue of payment was removed. It was agreed, therefore, that if a young person was found to be either 'vulnerable' under the Housing Act or 'in need' under the Children Act, then housing and social services would split the cost 50:50.

Jointly agreed criteria

Although the Housing Act 1996 did not take the opportunity to develop a joint definition of 'vulnerable' and 'in need', it is possible for housing and social services departments to agree on interpretations of the legislation that complement each other, or to draw up joint criteria. These should be flexible enough to enable either department to exercise discretion. If jointly agreed criteria are adopted it will make joint assessments significantly more straightforward, and improve service delivery.

Oxford City Council housing department and Oxfordshire social services' jointly agreed criteria for defining 'child in need', 'vulnerability', 'seriously prejudiced' and 'homeless'

The following criteria are used to establish if a young person is a child in need/vulnerable:

i)   child at risk of violence

ii) child at risk of emotional or sexual abuse

iii) child at risk of financial or sexual exploitation

iv) child at risk of severe conflict in home situation e.g. drugs, psychiatric illness in parents etc

v)   child at risk of severe neglect i.e. responsible adults unable to provide reasonable standards of diet, physical care including medical care, stimulation, social contact, educational support, stability/security, warmth/affection

vi) child with a disability — learning difficulty, sensory disorder, communication disorder, challenging behaviour (conduct disorders), motor disorders, chronic illness, terminal illness and psychiatric illness

The following criteria are used to establish whether a young person is homeless and if their welfare will be seriously prejudiced if accommodation is not provided:

i)   no responsible adult willing to provide suitable accommodation

ii) young person has been physically or sexually abused within current accommodation

iii) young person has been evicted or will be evicted within 28 days

iv) young person is escaping from severe conflict within current accommodation, e.g. drugs, violence etc

v)   young person about to leave institutions e.g. penal institutions

Role of advocacy services

Young people are often reluctant to ask for help, especially from statutory authorities. Legal terminology and the need to undergo assessments can dissuade them further. Advocacy services can greatly assist young people when they are at a crisis point in their lives and can form part of a joint protocol. (See chapter 6 for more details.)

If a young person has an advocate it can also assist the local authority in discharging its duties. An independent body will assist with communication and understanding and help ensure consistent treatment. An advocate will explain to the young person what to expect when they approach the local authority, and outline the kind of questions that will be asked. This should help them feel more relaxed and prepared, so that the interview will run more smoothly and save time. They will also have an understanding of their rights and realistic expectations about the service they can expect. It is clearly most appropriate that advocacy is provided by an independent agency, possibly funded by the local authority.

Centre 33, Cambridge: A voluntary agency providing an advocacy service for young people

Centre 33 is a voluntary agency providing counselling and information to young people. In 1994, it set up an advocacy service for homeless or potentially homeless 16 and 17-year-olds, in response to an increasing number of approaches from young people in housing need. This involved explaining in detail their rights under both the Housing Act and the Children Act, and accompanying them for assessments if necessary.

The worker also accompanied young people to the Benefits Agency to secure income support and crisis payments. This work fed into a Children Act protocol developed and adopted by all the key agencies in the city. Centre 33 now works with a wider range of young people, not just 16 and 17-year-olds. This includes young carers, those at risk or involved in the criminal justice system, those facing exclusion or excluded from school, and those leaving care or without appropriate adult support.

☐ Implications of the Children Act for housing benefit eligibility

If a young person is found to be a 'child in need' under the Children Act, this has implications for their eligibility for housing benefit. This issue is discussed in detail in Chapter 8.

☐ Allocation of social housing

It is crucial that young people's long-term housing requirements are taken into account when their needs are being assessed. One source of permanent accommodation is social housing accessed through the housing register and allocation system. This section explores the legal responsibilities and good practice in allocating housing.

The housing register

Note that revised Codes of Guidance are due for publication in England and Wales in 1998, so the following paragraph references and some of the content may be changed.

Section 162(1) of the Housing Act 1996 states: "Every local authority shall establish and maintain a register of qualifying persons (their 'housing register')." **Section 161(1)** states: "A local housing authority shall allocate housing accommodation only to persons ('qualifying person') who are qualified to be allocated housing accommodation by that authority."

Certain categories of people must be allowed to appear on the housing register:

- A person over the age of 18 who is owed a duty by the authority under section 193 (i.e. homeless); or under section 195(2) (threatened homelessness)
- A person over the age of 18 years who has within the previous two years been owed a duty under section 192(2) (not in priority need), or section 197(2) (duty where other accommodation is available)

Those who are not allowed to appear on the housing register include:

- Persons subject to immigration control, unless they fall within a list of specified exceptions
- Some persons from abroad who are not qualifying persons

(Codes of Guidance on Parts VI and VII of the Housing Act 1996, **paragraph 4.6.**)

Section 161(4) of the Act states that: "A local housing authority may decide what classes of persons are, or are not, qualifying persons." In deciding who is a 'qualifying person', local authorities are exhorted not to draw the classes so tightly as to exclude people who may be in housing need.

Authorities should not exclude young people from the housing register solely on the basis of age. Nor should authorities make a distinction between single young people and young couples. **Paragraph 4.26** of the Code of Guidance states: "There is a considerable range of practice among local authorities in the use of minimum age limits for acceptance onto a waiting list. In deciding whether, and if so where, to set an age limit, local authorities will want to bear in mind the needs of vulnerable young single people, such as care leavers, who may need a long-term tenancy." Local housing authorities should liaise with social services departments regarding care leavers in particular. In many situations young people are expected to leave care at age 16 or 17, but are not allowed onto the housing register until they are 18.

If a young person has been excluded from the housing register they have a right to request a review when there is a class of qualifying persons into which he or she believes he fits **(section 164)**. The local housing authority also still has a duty to make enquiries if they have reason to believe the young person is homeless or threatened with homelessness **(section 184)**. In some cases, the authority may have a duty to secure temporary accommodation for the young person while those enquiries are carried out.

The situation in Scotland is significantly different. A recent report (Anderson and Morgan, 1997) highlights the differences between Scotland and England and Wales with regard to housing registers and allocations: "Under Scottish legislation, all young people are eligible to apply for council housing and hold a tenancy from the age of 16. In England and Wales, age restrictions on eligibility to join the housing list and to be allocated a tenancy continue to discriminate against young people." The report goes on to say that the critical differentiation was between the treatment of those aged 16 and 17 and those aged 18 and over. Only half of English and Welsh authorities allowed 16-year-olds to register on the housing list, and nearly a third denied access to households with children where the parent was less than 18 years old.

Allocations

The framework for the allocation of permanent housing is laid down in section 167 of the Housing Act 1996. The allocation scheme must be framed to ensure that 'reasonable preference' is given to a variety of groups of people:

(a) People occupying insanitary or overcrowded housing or otherwise living in unsatisfactory housing conditions

(b) People occupying housing accommodation which is temporary or occupied on insecure terms

(c) Families with dependent children

(d) Households consisting of or including someone who is expecting a child

(e) Households consisting of or including someone with a particular need for settled accommodation on medical or welfare grounds

(f) Households whose social or economic circumstances are such that they have difficulty in securing settled accommodation

(g) People owed a homelessness duty under section 193 or 195(2) of the Housing Act 1996; people accommodated beyond the two-year period under section 194; and those accommodated by means of advice and assistance under section 197, or who have been provided with advice and assistance within the previous two years

Depending on their individual circumstances, young people could fall into any of these subsections. The 1996 Code of Guidance refers to the needs of young people in a number of places **(Note that revised Codes of Guidance are due for publication in England and Wales in 1998, so the following paragraph references may be changed)**:

Paragraph 5.13 offers guidance on the meaning of 'welfare grounds' as referred to in category (e) above: "[They] are intended to encompass not only care and support needs, but also other social needs which do not require ongoing care and support, such as the need to provide a secure base from which a care leaver or other vulnerable person can build a stable life."

Paragraph 5.15 refers to those found to be a 'child in need' under the Children Act: "A child in need may be a person with a need for settled accommodation on medical or welfare grounds: housing authorities are unlikely to be able to reach a decision on the level of priority to accord such cases without taking into account the views of the social services authority."

Paragraph 5.19 states that category (f) "reflects the particular difficulties that some households on a low income may have in obtaining settled accommodation for themselves in the private sector. Local authorities should consider both the household's immediate circumstances and its longer-term prospects." This is particularly relevant for young people under the age of 25 who are subject to the single room restriction of their housing benefit entitlement.

Section 167 of the Housing Act 1996 also states that 'additional preference' should be given to someone who falls within subsection (e) and cannot reasonably be expected to find settled accommodation for themselves in the foreseeable future. **Paragraph 5.11** (paragraph 5.10 in Wales) of the Code of Guidance states that: "Close and effective working between housing, social services and health authorities will be critical in order to deliver the most appropriate solution to the housing, support and care needs of people who come into this category."

In allocating housing accommodation, local authorities should take into account nomination arrangements with housing associations. These can be used imaginatively, for example, to provide move-on units.

Authorities can also set aside a quota of allocations for specific groups provided that this is set out in their allocation scheme. **Paragraph 5.22** (paragraph 5.26 in Wales) of the Code of Guidance says: "Many authorities have in the past made arrangements that effectively set aside a quota of anticipated allocations for groups with particular characteristics, and in some cases allocate the accommodation on the basis of referrals from social services departments, welfare bodies or specialised agencies dealing with rough sleepers. Establishing such quotas can form part of an authority's strategy to integrate the provision of housing with other social policies, for example … to enable individuals to move on from a hostel providing temporary accommodation."

Although it may be appropriate to set aside a quota of allocations for young people, this should not mean earmarking certain areas or estates (unless this forms part of a specific strategy and is appropriately managed — see Knowsley case study, chapter 4). Young people should be given the same level of choice as any other applicant.

Young people's individual needs should be also be taken into account. This obviously covers health and disability, but should go beyond these. Does the young person need to live in a particular area? Do they need to be near training establishments, or on a public transport route? Appropriate allocations will increase the likelihood of the tenancy succeeding.

☐ Conclusion and checklist

The Housing Act and Children Act are two crucial tools in assisting young people in housing need. It is of paramount importance that the duties embodied in the Acts are fulfilled and the powers used to the benefit of young people. To do this effectively housing and social services departments must work together, and with other agencies. Both departments must jointly take responsibility for the young people in the area. If young people's needs are not addressed at an early stage they will simply return at a later stage when they have become more chronic, and more expensive.

> In joint working under the Housing Act and Children Act, it is important to:
> - Ensure housing and social services staff are familiar with both the Housing Act and Children Act and the Secretary of State's guidance, and that they are kept up to date with any changes in legislation or guidance
> - Develop joint working between social services and housing departments:
>   - joint planning
>   - joint protocols and procedures
>   - joint assessments
>   - jointly agreed definitions
> - Include the voluntary sector and other agencies in this joint work
> - Include frontline workers in developing these joint approaches to ensure they are appropriate and properly implemented
> - Consider treating young people automatically as in 'priority need' by virtue of their age
> - Develop, or support the development of, an independent advocacy service
> - Allow young people onto the housing register, particularly care leavers
> - Ensure young people are not discriminated against in the allocation system. Ensure they have the same level of choice as others

CHAPTER 6

Prevention and Preparation

☐ Introduction

Preventative and preparative work is an essential part of any housing strategy for young people. Although the average age of leaving home in the UK is 21 for men and 20 for women (British Youth Council, 1996), many of the young people who find themselves homeless or in poor housing conditions have been forced to leave much earlier. Not only have few had any training or guidance in independent living, but at such a young age many do not have the skills or resources to cope.

Young people need to know what accommodation is available; what benefits they can claim; and the right information they should give to agencies and services. They need support, and they also need the appropriate expectations and life skills to maintain a tenancy. Those who would like to rebuild a relationship with their families and perhaps even return home often need a third party to make this possible.

Lacking these skills and support networks, many young people find themselves in damaging and difficult situations. As a result, they become disillusioned, increasingly mistrustful of authority and excluded from society. As they are pushed further away from the mainstream, their expectations may become unrealistic, which in turn worsens their exclusion.

This chapter looks at advice and information services; advocacy; preparation for independence work through peer education; early intervention work; social services' role in relation to care leavers; and mediation services.

☐ Advice and information

The Housing Act imposes a statutory duty on local authorities to provide advice to homeless people and those threatened with homelessness. The provision of good quality, easily-accessible information should be a priority for any housing strategy.

Range of advice and information

Young people need information and advice about these core areas:

- Accommodation available in the area
- Accessing accommodation
- Private sector landlords
- Tenancy rights, especially in the private sector
- Rights under the Housing Act 1996, Housing (Scotland) Act 1987, Housing Act 1988, Housing Act (Scotland) 1988 or Housing (Northern Ireland) Order 1988 and the Children Act 1989, Children (Scotland) Act 1995 or Children (Northern Ireland) Order 1995
- Benefit entitlement: housing benefit, Jobseeker's Allowance, income support, severe hardship payments, crisis loans, community care grants
- Availability of payments under the Children Act

Additional areas that an advice and information service could cover include:

- Budgeting skills
- Employment and training opportunities
- Relationships and sexuality
- Health education, including drugs and alcohol
- Managing friends and neighbours
- Job-seeking skills or other basic skills

If the advice service concentrates on housing and benefits it should be able to direct young people to appropriate services dealing with these other issues, as well as counselling services.

Young people are in the best position to advise on what information and advice should be provided. If the service is still being developed, they should be consulted at this stage (see chapter 2). If it is already up and running, they can be consulted through:

- Exit questionnaires

- A suggestion box
- Focus groups, both of existing users and the general population of young people

Access to advice and information services

Publicity: Young people must be made aware of advice and information services. Local newspapers, radio and television may carry paid advertising or articles. Leaflets and posters should be distributed widely, kept up to date and replaced when necessary. An outreach worker or volunteers may be used to visit schools and youth clubs. This personal contact will often encourage young people who are unsure about approaching such services. Publicity should also be targeted at other professionals such as doctors, health visitors and teachers.

Location and transport: Services need to be located so that young people can get to them. Transport to services should form an integral part of a strategic plan.

Freephone advice line: If transport is problematic, one solution may be a telephone advice line. This should be a freephone number if possible or it may be worth advertising the fact that it is possible to call the young person back once they have contacted the advice line.

Mobile provision: This can serve a wide range of communities, but it may not be in each location very often. It is crucial to advertise when the service is going to be where.

The Van, Oxfordshire

The Van, a mobile advice and information service launched in 1993, serves the rural areas of Oxfordshire, providing information and advice on a range of issues as well as housing. The project is managed by Oxfordshire Association of Young People and is primarily funded by the Oxfordshire health authority with donations from trusts and charities. Young people were consulted during the development phase through questionnaires about the kind of service they wanted and the areas it should visit.

The Van contains a computer running the Heart of England TEC Training Access Point programme, which enables users to investigate all training opportunities in the surrounding area, and the Lisson Grove Welfare Benefits programme, which enables them to work out their benefit entitlements. The project has a mobile phone so that young people can refer themselves to specialist agencies. All young people who use the Van are asked to complete an anonymous monitoring form.

Relevant services: Services should be part of the local network and structure. Young people in rural areas may have particular problems identifying with services based in the town, however easily they can be reached. If services for these young people cannot be based in rural areas it is important to be very explicit about their relevance.

Appropriate services: Accessibility goes beyond location and transport. Advice services need to be welcoming, easy places for young people to use. This does not necessarily mean a separate service for young people (although this may be the ideal), but service providers should make special efforts to consider young people's needs. Issues to consider when ensuring that a service is appropriate for young people include:

- What is the attitude of the staff?

- How knowledgeable are staff about young people's rights?

- What does the centre look like? How is it decorated?

- Is there a confidential waiting area and interview area?

Cynon Action for Single Homeless: A centrally-based project with a shop front

Cynon Action for Single Homeless (CASH) is based in Aberdare. In 1996, the project moved its central base to a shop front building, where it is felt that the accessibility and high profile of the new offices is partly responsible for a 63 per cent increase in the number of clients seeking information and advice.

In addition to providing advice and information, CASH also provides an accommodation scheme for seven young people aged 16-24; an education, training and employment project; the Doorstep scheme through which properties in the private sector are leased; and the New Start scheme which aims to meet the accommodation needs of all clients referred from the probation service.

Opening hours: It may be more important for an advice centre to be open during the late afternoon than during the day. Saturday morning opening can also make a significant difference, especially if the advice centre is based in the local shopping centre or town.

Time Stop, Peterborough: A comprehensive 24-hour service for young people

The Time Stop Project was developed by Peterborough YMCA for young people aged 16-25. It provides a 24-hour service throughout the year. The project is funded by Peterborough City Council, Cambridgeshire County Council, Cambridgeshire Probation Service, the Housing Corporation, the National Lottery Charities Board, other charitable trusts and public donations. Time Stop provides direct-access accommodation for up to three months; a free counselling service; a drop-in centre offering advice and information on all subjects; art and craft activities; sporting opportunities; a parents and toddlers group; pregnancy testing; and a coffee bar. In 1996, Time Stop started a training programme based on promoting numeracy and literacy skills and pre-vocational training, run jointly with Isle College in Wisbech and funded by the European Social Fund.

☐ Advocacy

In some cases, information and advice may not be enough to get young people access to services. This is particularly so when dealing with benefit claims or seeking an assessment under the Children Act or Housing Act (see chapter 5). It may therefore be necessary to provide an advocacy service.

What is an advocate? An advocate is someone who 'speaks in favour of another'. True advocacy is as much about enabling as representation. It is about changing the balance of power so that it is more evenly distributed, sharing information and knowledge with young people and enabling them to apply this knowledge in an appropriate way. Advocacy is different to the role played by a support worker. A support worker is responsible for the young person's resettlement or care plan and as such cannot be their advocate.

Who provides advocacy? Advocacy is provided most appropriately by an independent voluntary agency. It is extremely unlikely that an employee of the local authority could act successfully as an advocate, partly because their interests may conflict, but also because young people may not believe that they are impartial. Hostel staff cannot act as advocates on issues related to the young person's current accommodation, as they are employees of the young person's landlord. An advocate must be truly independent.

Effective advocacy: Effective advocacy enables the young person to express their own views more easily and negotiate their own needs; helps them make informed choices; accurately voices the needs and desires of the person being represented; and maintains an independent stance wherever possible. Advocates should always act in the client's best interests and in accordance with their wishes and instructions; keep the client properly informed; act impartially; offer frank, independent advice; and maintain client confidentiality.

Clarity of role and purpose: When an advocacy service is established, it is important that all parties are clear about its role and purpose. The advocacy service should liaise with the organisations it will be working with to ensure that this takes place. Advocacy is not about enabling the young person to fulfil unrealistic expectations. Nor is it about encouraging a young person to accept an unsuitable solution.

Before accompanying a young person to an agency, an advocate should make their role clear to the young person. It is not necessarily the advocate's job to do the talking; a meeting with an advocate present should never become a meeting between two professionals, bypassing the young person.

☐ Preparation for independence

Schools-based work

The Education Reform Act (1988) places on schools in England and Wales a statutory responsibility to "prepare pupils for the opportunities, responsibilities and experiences of adult life". The National Curriculum Guidance (Guidance 3, The Whole Curriculum) talks about "preparing young people to take their place in a wide range of roles in adult life" and asserts that the core and foundation subjects in the national curriculum will not necessarily provide the necessary breadth for a pupil's school education. The Guidance also recommends "recognising and defining the nature of a problem — for example, homelessness" and a specific unit of work around the "causes, benefits and disadvantages of leaving home ... identifying the various options open to those who leave home including sources of help" (Guidance 8, Education for Citizenship).

'Preparation for independence' is a broad term. The work can look simply at leaving home and securing accommodation. It can go on to look at the related issues of income, training, employment and budgeting skills; and lead on to household skills and practical matters such as obtaining furniture. The work can also address broader independent living skills such as self-esteem, confidence, assertiveness and negotiation skills. In order to deliver this work successfully, schools, colleges and the education authority need to work jointly with housing and other appropriate agencies.

Learning to negotiate, compromise and live on a limited budget is important for all young people leaving home, not simply those leaving care or at risk of becoming homeless. The decision whether to work with a whole year group or to target young people at risk will depend on the age group, the skills and resources available and the identified need.

Lambeth: Targeted schools-based work

In 1996, Centrepoint's education team began a year-long project working in two Lambeth schools, building on some existing provision to facilitate preparing for leaving home. The work was developed not just in personal and social education but also in sociology, drama and the youth award scheme. Instead of a fixed model or programme, teachers were supported in devising their own.

Young people were involved in design and delivery of this work, particularly through a pupil referral centre, where some young people organised visits to housing projects for other pupils. Regular monitoring established which groups of young people were reached and how. The project was successful in raising teachers' awareness and developing work in both curriculum and non-curriculum areas. It managed both to target young people at risk in a mainstream environment and to work successfully in the non-mainstream setting of a pupil referral unit.

Teaching material and 'leaving-home' guides

Many housing organisations have worked successfully with schools to develop teaching materials for teachers and 'leaving-home' guides for young people. This has often been funded by building societies. Existing packs can be adapted for local use.

Colchester: A leaving-home project which has involved young people extensively in producing resources

Colchester Borough Council's housing advice centre and the local night shelter have been operating a leaving-home project in secondary schools for a number of years. The project has produced a teaching pack for use in schools and a youth pack for youth clubs.

→

Young people have been extensively involved and consulted about what they require. The leaving-home youth pack was developed with the help of all secondary and special schools in the borough. It consists of students' art, poetry and essays, as well as data on housing and homelessness. Homeless people were given single-use cameras to record impressions of a week in their lives, and the local college produced a video which features interviews with homeless people and uses theme music recorded by a local school. The project's effectiveness is continually monitored through focus groups and evaluation sheets.

Peer education

Peer education, in which young people educate other young people, based on their personal experiences, has been used extensively in health education. It can also be an appropriate way for young people to discuss issues such as leaving home and independent living in a range of settings and environments.

Centrepoint: A peer education project working with young people who are or have recently been homeless

Centrepoint, in conjunction with Grimethorpe Activity Zone, Platform GFS and Sandwell Housing and Resettlement Project, has developed peer education work with young people who are or have recently been homeless. Four groups are involved around the country, and the project has evolved very differently within each one. The London-based group of Centrepoint residents and ex-residents developed a video and a range of activities for use in schools and youth clubs; the Grimethorpe group of young people from an area of disadvantage and high unemployment developed drama work; the Swindon group of homeless young women developed a video and art-based work; and the Sandwell group of homeless young people developed an interactive session using quizzes and games.

Feedback from young people attending peer-led sessions indicate that peer education by homeless or recently homeless young people can be very appropriate and effective. It has had a demonstrable impact on the lives of the peer educators, their personal and social skills and their employment opportunities.

☐ Early intervention

Estate-based work

Social housing estates often contain a high concentration of people who are socially deprived (Page, 1993). Research carried out for the Joseph Rowntree Foundation (Lee and Murie, 1997) showed that "the national trend for disadvantaged households to gravitate towards council housing and the social rented sector generally applies at a local level". The obvious corollary of this is that young people on estates should be provided with information, skills and support to reduce their likelihood of becoming homeless. Estate-based work can also help to improve the living environment of the estate.

However, the Rowntree research also found that "Disadvantaged groups are not exclusively housed in the social rented sector or in council housing. The associations between housing tenure and disadvantaged households differ between different cities" — with deprivation sometimes widespread outside the social rented sector. It is crucial, therefore, that the decision about where to target work is made locally, and looks beyond social housing estates to other areas of deprivation.

Applications for housing

Homelessness and the need for rehousing can be reduced by improving the advice and support young people receive when they first approach the local housing authority, either to enquire about homelessness or to register for housing. Early intervention can open up a number of options, such as family reconciliation. Similarly, establishing the reasons why tenancies break down can assist in providing appropriate services in future.

First Move, Newcastle: An early warning and screening process for young people likely to become homeless

First Move is a joint council and voluntary sector team set up in 1991 after advice workers found increasing numbers of young people giving up tenancies following the 1988 benefit cuts. It was also a response to the introduction of the Children Act 1989, which envisaged greater responsibility and flexibility from council services. The team is joint-funded by Barnados, the housing department and the health authority, with six staff seconded from social services.

→

The First Move team and the housing department established an early warning and screening process for young people likely to become homeless. In 1993, an examination of rehousing applications indicated that many homeless young people had applied to the housing department neighbourhood offices some time before they became homeless. First Move began to contact all those young people who had approached the local housing office, offering independent advice and continuing support. Around 120 young people have used these services each year, reducing the number of single homeless young people needing rehousing.

Developing out of this work, a study in 1994-96 identified the factors determining the success or failure of an independent tenancy after a young person leaves home or care, and established young people's views on existing provision and the need for other support. It is now proposed to extend First Move's work to other vulnerable young people.

☐ Role of social services

Young people leaving care are expected to make the transition to independence at a much younger age than others. Around two-thirds have left care by their eighteenth birthday (Evans, 1996). Young people who have been in care are particularly vulnerable to homelessness. Centrepoint figures (1997) show that 24 per cent of residents had experienced being 'looked after' by a local authority, although only one per cent of all children and young people under the age of 18 have been in care (Evans, 1996).

Preparation for young people leaving care

Social services departments have a legal obligation to advice, assist and befriend young people "with a view to promoting their welfare when they cease to be looked after" (Children Act 1989, section 24; Children (Scotland) Act 1995, section 17; Children (Northern Ireland) Order 1995). Homelessness legislation guidance states that care leavers' housing needs should be addressed before they leave care, and arrangements should be made for joint assessment between social services and housing departments (Housing Act 1996 Code of Guidance, paragraph 14.11; Housing (Scotland) Act 1987 Code of Guidance 1997, paragraph 4.17). If young people are encouraged to remain in care until they are ready to make the transition to independent living they are far less likely to become homeless. Social services must therefore fulfil their obligation to prepare young people for their transition to independence and ensure that they leave care at an appropriate stage.

Box 6a: Standards in Leaving Care

The national leaving-care advisory service, First Key, set up a working group to produce standards in leaving care (1996). These standards set out the following checklist:

1. The social services department has a clearly written, accessible and comprehensive leaving care policy statement which is fully integrated into the local authority children's services plan.

2. The child care policy statement relating to leaving care is put into operation through written procedures and practice guidance, which are actively promoted within the department.

3. Throughout the development and delivery of services to young people leaving care, the social services department and other leaving-care service providers promote anti-discriminatory work with young black people.

4. The social services department should have continuous planning processes, which take account of the past, current and future needs of all individual young people.

5. The social services department ensures that the individual planning process is comprehensive.

6. The social services department planning process takes particular account of the financial support from the department that will need to be available to young people.

7. The social services department and other leaving-care service providers' decision-making process allows for full involvement and contribution by the young person, and takes account of the pace of change and implementation appropriate to the young person.

8. The social services department and other leaving-care service providers have in place an appropriately staffed and managed service, based upon a clear model, for after-care services. The component parts of the service are clearly costed and specified within the local authority budget-making process and are reviewed on an annual basis.

→

9. Where a specialist model of service delivery is used, it is integrated and designed to complement and extend care services rather than replace them.

10. The social services department and other leaving-care service providers have a clear management strategy in place for training and developing all staff and carers involved in developing, delivering and administering leaving-care services.

11. The social services department ensures that a 'leaving care guide' is produced and provided for those young people eligible for services.

12. The local authority has in place a corporate and inter-agency framework agreed through formal committee and planning structures.

13. The social services department and other leaving-care service providers have in place formal joint working arrangements with all accommodation providers — including housing departments and housing associations — to ensure that a range of safe and affordable accommodation options are available to meet the needs of care leavers. Housing departments take a lead role in enabling an overall accommodation strategy.

14. The social services department and other leaving-care service providers have formal joint working arrangements in place with education, employment and training providers to ensure access to appropriate programmes.

15. The social services department and other leaving-care service providers have joint working arrangements in place with local benefit agencies to ensure that young people receive their full financial entitlements and that the process of obtaining such entitlements is streamlined and provides direct access.

16. Those agencies providing services to care leavers have procedures which enable young people, parents, carers and other significant people to make representations, including complaints, about any aspect of the leaving-care service.

17. Those agencies providing services to care leavers have systems in place for monitoring services and evaluating the outcomes. The findings of these systems are utilised in future service design and development.

Source: First Key, 1996

Young people leaving care should have the option of returning to accommodation provided by social services. This may be necessary if they left care too early or if they are subsequently faced with homelessness. It is very important that care leavers are given more than one chance.

Supported accommodation or 'floating support' schemes enable a staged transition to full independence for young people who have been looked after by social services (see chapter 7).

Foster care initiatives

Many housing problems result from young people being forced to leave home before they are ready to live independently. Nearly half of the 16 and 17-year-olds arriving at Centrepoint's emergency shelter said they had first run away from home before their sixteenth birthday (Centrepoint, 1996). It may not be possible or appropriate for young people to remain in the family home. It is important, therefore, to have other options, including foster care.

Newcastle City Council: Recruitment of additional foster carers for older teenagers

Newcastle City Council found that insufficient foster care for young people aged 15 and over was leading indirectly to an increase in homelessness. Without enough appropriate foster care young people were being given independent accommodation too soon, and their tenancies were breaking down.

This link was highlighted by:

- discussions amongst colleagues;
- a cohort study of young people informing joint social services and housing strategy;
- records of homeless young people: every young person presenting as homeless undergoes a detailed interview to ascertain their history and track back to the initial 'cause'.

In response to this, social services set up a new fostering support and development team to recruit more foster parents for older teenagers. Allowances to foster carers are also being reviewed.

After-care

In addition to preparing young people for the transition from care to independence, social services departments have a responsibility to advise and befriend care-leavers if they ask for help until they reach the age of 21 (Children Act 1989, section 24; Children (Scotland) Act 1995, section 29; Children (Northern Ireland) Order 1995, article 21).

☐ Mediation work

Some young people leave home after the relationship with their family breaks down. Some relationships will be irreparable, at least for a period of time. Others can be salvaged, but not to the point where the young person can or will return home. Some young people may wish to return, however, but be unable to negotiate that return on their own.

Mediation services can help young people make contact with their families again and reach agreement about the way forward. Meetings can be face-to-face or 'shuttle' arrangements (so participants do not have to meet directly), and participants are enabled to reach mutually acceptable arrangements. Confidentiality issues must be fully discussed before mediation begins.

Family Mediating Service: A mediation service for homeless young people

The Family Mediating Service (FMS) was developed by Alone in London, an organisation providing a range of services to young people who are or may become homeless. Fifty-nine per cent of young people using the service cited family breakdown as the major cause of their homelessness; and of these, 56 per cent said they would welcome the chance to work at repairing family relationships.

FMS provides a range of services in addition to mediation. Contact work supporting young people, or on their behalf, enables them to rebuild their relationship with their family. A PO Box address is available so that young people can receive correspondence without giving an address. One-to-one work allows young people to spend time talking about their family situation, possibly with a view to identifying strategies for family work. FMS will also refer young people to other services if appropriate.

Mediation is provided by a team of trained and experienced volunteers who initially meet the young person to explain the process and talk about confidentiality. Either face-to-face meeting or shuttle mediation may be appropriate. Meetings take place at neutral venues. Mediation can be used to negotiate a range of outcomes. Young people are involved in a full feedback procedure that includes assessing the project and contributing to new developments.

☐ Conclusion and checklist

Providing a fence at the top of a cliff is better than providing an ambulance at the bottom. Prevention saves young people from ending up in traumatic crisis situations and helps them to experience a smooth transition to independence, which gives them a solid grounding for their adult life. It also means agencies do not have to carry out lengthy and expensive remedial work.

A young people's housing strategy must include:

- Advice and information services. Young people should be consulted to establish the range of topics these services cover. Services must be made accessible to young people through advertising; appropriate geographical location, possibly including a freephone service or mobile provision; and appropriate delivery, including opening hours.

- Advocacy services to ensure that young people are able to exercise their rights. The purpose and expectations of these services must be made clear.

- Work across the schools curriculum whenever possible, focusing on preparation for independence. Specific work targeted at those most at risk of homelessness should also be considered. Housing agencies can work with schools to develop teaching materials and leaving-home guides.

- Peer education work, where appropriate, including work with young people who have been homeless.

- Early intervention work in areas of high deprivation, particularly through youth work.

- Appropriate advice for young people applying to be put on the housing register or making a homelessness inquiry.

- Social services arrangements preparing young people in care for the transition to independence, and providing appropriate accommodation and support, including foster care and floating support.

- The option of mediation services that have been developed specifically for work with homeless young people.

CHAPTER 7

Housing Management and Support

☐ Introduction

The service and support a young person receives in conjunction with their accommodation is crucial. If the core service is not appropriately delivered or sufficiently supported, no degree of strategic planning and multi-agency working will help. Not only should needs be assessed at a strategic level to ensure appropriate service planning, but each individual's needs should be assessed when they access a service. The more responsive and appropriate the accommodation and support, the more likely the young person is to succeed in the property and be able to make it their home.

This chapter looks at the provision of appropriate accommodation and in particular at Nightstop or stopover schemes and private rented sector initiatives. It also covers differing legal opinions about occupancy agreements; the allocation of independent accommodation to young people; maintaining tenancies; tenant participation; the implications of welfare benefits and the New Deal; and a range of ways of providing support, including supported accommodation, floating support, supported lodgings and starter packs.

☐ Management or support

There is no definitive answer about what is management and what is support; the boundaries are blurred. A useful distinction, developed for floating support by CVS Consultants, can be applied more broadly and should be used as a frame of reference when reading this chapter (see Box 7a).

Box 7a: Definitions of basic housing management, intensive housing management, support and care

Basic housing management	Intensive housing management	Support	Care
Rent and service charge collection	Rent and service charge collection		
Taking action on arrears	Taking action on arrears		
Selection and allocation	Selection and allocation		
Transfers, mutual exchanges, voids	Transfers, mutual exchanges, voids		
Tenancy agreements and tenant rights	Tenancy agreements and tenant rights		
Repairs and maintenance	Repairs and maintenance		
Consultation with tenants	Consultation with tenants		
Dealing with tenant disputes	Dealing with tenant disputes		
	Advice on move-on		
	Advice on aids and adaptations		
	Advice on claiming housing benefit	Advice on welfare benefits	
	Advice on bills and debts re tenancy	Advice on all debts	
	Advice on care and support services	Advocacy on accessing care/support services	
	Encouraging contact with these services	Accompanying tenants	
	Contacting relatives or care services directly	Close contact with relatives/care services	
	Advice on dealing with police re tenancy	Advice on dealing with police on all matters	
	Occasional temporary help with care/support	Life skills training	
		Practical help and support	
		Drawing up and reviewing individual support plans	
		Advising on community facilities	
		Providing education or training	
		Counselling on personal and emotional problems	Specialist counselling/therapy
			Personal care
			Domiciliary help
			Medical treatment
			Nursing care
			Providing education or training

Source: CVS Consultants (1997)

☐ Provision of appropriate accommodation

It is important to provide a range of accommodation for young people, from direct-access, short-term provision through temporary and medium-term projects to permanent accommodation. This accommodation can take a variety of forms, from hostels and Nightstop/stopover schemes, supported housing projects and access to the private rented sector to permanent tenancies in social housing. The full range of provision is not discussed in detail here as many of the options are not specific to young people. Supported housing options are discussed later in the chapter. Nightstop/stopover schemes, which are specifically designed for young people, and private rented sector initiatives are discussed below.

Nightstop/stopover schemes

Nightstop schemes provide emergency accommodation for young homeless single people between the ages of 16 and 25 in the homes of a network of volunteer hosts, families and individuals. The Nightstop name is a patented trademark of the Nightstop National Network. Although not patented, similar emergency accommodation schemes for young people in several Scottish towns and cities are known as 'stopovers'. This sort of scheme may be particularly useful in places where there is no hostel provision or no appropriate hostels, such as in rural areas.

Nightstop/stopover schemes may seem an attractive option as they involve no capital expenditure, since they make use of householders' spare rooms. Like any other scheme, however, they need careful planning, management and monitoring, and sufficient revenue funding. Most existing Nightstop schemes are funded through section 180 grants from the DETR, charitable sources, local authorities and occasionally the Department of Health. Factors that need to be taken into account in developing this type of service include:

- Geographical area of operation
- Referral agencies
- Confidentiality
- Police checks of hosts
- Personal liability insurance
- Recruitment, vetting and training of hosts
- Ongoing training, support and development
- Follow up work with young people

Leeds Accommodation Project Nightstop scheme

Leeds Accommodation Project is a Barnardo's project working with homeless young people and care leavers. It provides three services: Nightstop, supported lodgings and a befriending scheme. Nightstop hosts offer accommodation in their own home for up to seven nights to a young person who has come through the Nightstop referral system. They are required to provide an evening meal and breakfast, to offer emotional support and to assist the young person in returning to the referring agency. Expenses are covered and they receive training, supervision and a wide range of information, on subjects including:

- Violence to volunteers and providers
- The young person's personal files
- Self-harm guidelines for accommodation providers
- Alcohol, drug taking and solvent abuse
- Health and safety standards
- Emergency medical treatment
- Equal opportunities
- Insurance cover
- Volunteer complaints

Private rented sector initiatives

The majority of young people seeking accommodation use the private rented sector (Spafford, 1994). However, tenancies are less secure in this sector; the quality of management and repair may be inferior and the rents higher than in the social sector; and young people may be vulnerable to harassment (Griffiths, 1997). Agencies have a key role, therefore, in enabling young people to access safe accommodation and to maintain their tenancy successfully. Clearly the introduction of single-room rent restrictions for the majority of single people under the age of 25 has had a major impact on access, but that does not diminish the value of these arrangements. Indeed, it makes them all the more relevant (see chapter 8).

The local authority housing department and other agencies should hold an up-to-date register of private rented accommodation. This register should only contain agencies or properties that are recommended and inspected by the authority. If the register is broader in scope, recommended agencies and properties should be indicated. When referring young people to private rented accommodation, the local authority or agency needs to be aware of their own legal liability in the event of subsequent harm to them, due to the standard of accommodation. Best practice suggests that local authorities should establish a landlord accreditation scheme.

They should also consider setting up a landlord forum. This provides a place where landlords can meet with the local authority and other relevant agencies to develop a common understanding, protocols and procedures, resolve difficulties and organise training. It should also provide individual landlords with support, thereby encouraging their continuing willingness to accommodate young people.

> The **Open Doors Project** in Croydon refers landlords of empty properties to one of four named accommodation agencies, which will take tenants in housing need. The agencies vet both the landlords and properties, and the local authority vets the agencies and the tenants.

☐ Occupancy agreements for 16 and 17-year-olds

This section does not apply in Scotland. Under Scottish law 16 and 17-year-olds are entitled to hold tenancies.

There is considerable confusion about the legal position on granting 16 and 17-year-olds occupancy rights. This confusion often prevents social landlords from accommodating care leavers and other 16 and 17-year-olds (Housing Corporation Circular 05/96). This section explores the differing opinions. Landlords are advised to seek legal advice if they need further information.

Tenancies held in trust

Luba and Fullwood (1996) state that there is no legal prohibition against granting a tenancy to a person under 18. Such an agreement is one of the few forms of contractual agreement with a minor that is legally enforceable. Legal difficulties arise only when the grant of the tenancy is applied.

Section 1(6) of the Law of Property Act 1925 states that a person under 18 cannot hold a legal estate in land, such as a tenancy. (A licence does not confer any interest in the land.) Therefore the grant of a tenancy cannot pass the legal interest to the young person. The young person gets the benefit of the grant (i.e. occupation of the premises as a licensee), but does not hold the tenancy. The Settled Land Act 1925 provides that the legal interest in the land — the tenancy — is vested in trustees to be held for the benefit of the young person. If a specific trust is not established then the landlord is deemed to hold the tenancy on trust for the young person.

Luba and Fullwood (1996) go on to say that tenancies held in trust give rise to difficulties, in particular over security of tenure. It is a requirement of a secure or assured (including assured shorthold) tenancy that the tenant is an individual and occupies the property as their home (Housing Act 1985 section 80, Housing Act 1988 section 1). The trustees, or the landlord in default, do not fulfil these conditions. If the landlord is holding the tenancy on trust "it faces the legal impossibility of serving notice on itself to try to bring the tenancy to an end". However, Shelter's view is that a landlord, including a local authority, can create a trust with itself and serve a notice to quit on itself.

The Housing Corporation (Circular 05/96) refers to the Law of Property Act: "The grant of a tenancy to a minor operates as a contract to hold the property in trust for him/her by the person granting the tenancy." The Corporation goes on to advise that "[Associations] should normally grant assured shorthold tenancies ... to young persons aged 16/17 until they reach their 18th birthday when they should normally be granted an assured periodic tenancy ... Associations should consider whether they should require an adult or other sponsoring organisation to guarantee that the minor meets the requirements of the tenancy agreement."

However, since a minor cannot hold a legal estate in land they cannot hold the tenancy. The tenancy is held in trust and the minor, who is the beneficiary of the trust, occupies the premises as a licensee. An individual or a corporate body can be a trustee. It is possible, therefore, for a landlord, or an individual who is not a minor, to act as trustee for a 16 or 17-year-old wishing to occupy accommodation. The trustee cannot fulfil the tenant condition of a secure or assured (including assured shorthold) tenancy, so a common law tenancy exists.

In addition to appointing a trustee, some landlords wish to appoint a third-party guarantor. The trustee and the guarantor can, but do not have to, be one and the same. The guarantor is usually used to ensure payment of rent and to cover any losses arising from the breach of other conditions of the tenancy agreement. Guarantors can prove valuable in assisting young people in maintaining their first tenancy. However, in cases where it is not possible to find anyone to act as a guarantor, a policy that requires a guarantor for 16 and 17-year-olds can produce problems.

Yorkshire Metropolitan Housing Association: An association that uses guarantors as part of a wider policy of providing support to 16 and 17-year-olds

Yorkshire Metropolitan housing association uses a third party to act as a guarantor in respect of tenancies for 16 and 17-year-olds. The guarantor, who may be the local authority, a voluntary organisation or an individual, plays the role of a trustee.

→

The guarantee covers rent and other breaches of tenancy. The young person is granted an assured or assured shorthold tenancy, to be reviewed after 12 months or on the date of the tenant's eighteenth birthday, whichever is sooner. This policy forms part of a wider policy for 16 and 17-year-olds, which places the emphasis on assessing and meeting support needs together with monitoring the success of their tenancies. Where 16 and 17-year-olds apply direct to the association, Yorkshire Metropolitan will approach social services to discuss their care and support needs.

Equitable tenancies

The Law Commission suggests that social landlords defer the grant of an actual legal tenancy until a young person reaches 18. Before the age of 18, the young person can occupy the property under an agreement for the future tenancy. In the interim, the young person has an 'equitable tenancy', and is liable for the rent and compliance with any conditions relating to terms of occupation. Luba and Fullwood (1996) state that this would be "sufficient to attract the protection of the Housing Acts".

Gill and Mogollon's (1996) view is that equitable tenancies have the advantage that landlords can treat minors in the same manner, granting them the same benefits and reserving the same rights, as adult tenants. There should be no uncertainty as to the legal status of the agreement, which will be of assistance in taking possession proceedings, and the complex provisions of the Settled Land Act 1925 do not apply.

However, Shelter's view is that while a minor may have a contract for an equitable tenancy, since they cannot hold a legal estate in land they will be occupying the premises as a licensee. This leads to uncertainty regarding the legal status of the agreement.

Swansea: An authority that uses equitable tenancies

Since reorganisation in April 1996, Swansea has issued equitable tenancies to all persons under the age of 18 who are allocated a council property. The young person signs for a tenancy in exactly the same way as someone aged over 18, but it is explained to them that they cannot legally hold the tenancy until they reach 18, so the authority will hold the tenancy in trust for them and grant them an equitable tenancy. It is also explained that this provides them with the same rights as other tenants and they will be treated in the same manner as other secure tenants. The arrangement becomes a normal secure tenancy at age 18.

Licences

Because of the confusion surrounding tenancies, many social landlords prefer to grant a licence to 16 and 17-year-olds. This is uncontroversial in situations where a licence is clearly appropriate, including shared accommodation (where the young person does not enjoy exclusive occupation) and serviced accommodation (where food, cleaning and laundering are provided). The Housing Corporation Circular 05/96 states that: "Licences should normally be used where accommodation is shared or the association provides personal services."

However, a licence is a different legal entity to a tenancy. The case of Street v Mountford (1985) made clear that if a purported licence gives an occupier exclusive possession of a property, for payment of rent, for a fixed or periodic term, then it would usually be regarded as a tenancy; but the judge in this case also made reference to "special circumstances ... which negatived the presumption of the tenancy". Shelter's view is that where the occupier is a minor this could be seen in court as a 'special circumstance'. Similarly, Luba and Fullwood (1996) state: "It has been argued that the courts will find agreements with young people to be licences because the legal ramifications of finding them to be tenancies are unclear and absurd."

Luba and Fullwood go on to discuss action against young licensees: "The courts will usually treat contractual licences as contracts for necessaries and therefore enforceable against minors. Indeed, contracts for lodgings have long been recognised as enforceable contracts under this classification. So a social landlord could certainly sue for an unpaid licence fee."

With regard to security, local authorities can grant secure licences. There is no equivalent assured or assured shorthold licence for housing associations or private sector landlords. However, the licence can contain contractual clauses for the benefit of the young person.

Starting Point, Belfast: A project providing services and therefore using licence agreements

In 1995, Starting Point opened a four-bedded house to provide residential care for young people aged 16-17. At present it is the only service of its kind in Northern Ireland. The Northern Ireland Housing Executive does not offer tenancies to young people aged under 18. Referrals to the project come from a variety of sources, including social services, the probation board and young people themselves. Young people are expected to stay for approximately three months during which time move-on accommodation is arranged. There is also one emergency bed. The project uses licence agreements as food is provided and staff have access to residents' rooms.

Legal action against young occupiers

If a young person defaults on payment or fails to comply with any of the conditions of occupation, the landlord can take legal action in the normal way (Luba and Fullwood, 1996). However, after issuing proceedings and before taking any further procedural steps, the landlord must apply to the court for the appointment of a *guardian ad litem* to look after the interests of the young person. This is usually a parent or social worker, but if no other suitable person is available, the role will be filled by the district judge of the county court in which the proceedings are brought. (See Housing Corporation Circular 05/96.)

Box 7b: Occupancy agreements for 16 and 17-year-olds — a summary

Licences

- Licences should be used where the accommodation is shared or services are provided.

- As a young person cannot hold a legal estate in land, it is arguable that even if they are granted a tenancy, they will be occupying the premises on a licence. Shelter recommends the use of licences that automatically mature (through a contractual clause) to a tenancy when the young person reaches the age of 18.

Tenancies

- Tenancies can be held in trust for a young person until they reach the age of 18. The young person receives the benefit of the grant of the tenancy and occupies the premises as a licensee. A guarantor can be used in addition to a trustee.

- The Law Commission recommends the use of an equitable tenancy until the young person reaches the age of 18. However, since a minor cannot hold a legal estate in land, it is arguable that they will be occupying the premises as a licensee.

- The Housing Corporation recommends the use of assured shorthold tenancies until the young person reaches the age of 18.

☐ Management

Allocating independent accommodation to young people

There is considerable debate about whether young people should be given independent accommodation or whether that is setting them up to fail, in a system that often does not allow them a second chance. In practice, it is not a simple matter of age but depends upon the individual. The important thing is to develop a system that is flexible and sensitive enough to be able to respond appropriately to each individual.

Young people should not be seen as an automatic management problem. Nor should they be discriminated against by allocation policies just because they are young (see chapter 5).

Maintaining tenancies

Young people need appropriate housing management to enable them to maintain their tenancies. This involves proactive management rather than waiting until problems have got to a stage where eviction is the only solution. If problems arise it is important to attempt to address the underlying causes. It may be beneficial to employ tenancy support workers, preferably with youth work backgrounds, to work specifically with young people.

Proactive management can encompass:

- Providing information in appropriate forms for young people
- Ensuring young people understand their rights
- Explaining systems for reporting repairs etc
- Intensive housing management
- Referring young people to appropriate services
- Consultation with young people

In order to fulfil these tasks, housing officers need to establish good working relationships with other frontline staff, such as social workers, advice workers and Employment Service staff.

If a young person has been given independent accommodation before they are able to manage it, they should be supported in making a managed move out of self-contained accommodation into more appropriate accommodation.

Cadwyn Housing Association: Proactive housing management to young people

In 1996, Cadwyn housing association appointed a tenancy support worker with a youth work background in response to an increasing number of homeless young people being referred to the association. The post is funded by Tai Cymru supported housing revenue grant. After two poorly-attended meetings were arranged for young tenants, it became apparent that they were reluctant to come to the association's offices, especially when they were expected to talk and might not feel they had anything to say.

→

Young people themselves arranged a third meeting, held at a local fast-food restaurant, resulting in a good turn out. This raised the following issues:

- Repairs: Many young people found it daunting to report repairs. This was fed back to the technical services manager and to the housing association board by the tenancy support worker.

- Security: Many young people felt insecure in their properties, and were particularly concerned about fire.

- Discrimination: Many young people felt they were discriminated against by other residents because of their age.

- Residents' newsletter: Young people felt the newsletter was of poor quality. They requested access to a computer so that they could write articles for the newsletter.

Tenant participation

Young people are notoriously under-represented in tenants' associations (Power and Tunstall, 1995). This means that social landlords need to take particular action to involve them. It may not be appropriate for young people to join the regular tenants' association; a separate youth forum may be more effective, at least initially, and the two groups can come together at a later stage. If they do not do so, it is important to ensure a good flow of information between them.

In areas where there is a limited amount of social housing, where it is dispersed across a wide area, or where there is no tradition of tenant involvement, good practice would suggest that landlords link up with existing youth work to involve young people.

Community Housing Association, Camden

Community Housing Association has appointed a youth and community development worker to work on its new 200-home development at Camden Goods Yard. The principal aim is to facilitate the creation of a youth forum to link in with the tenants' forum. It is anticipated that the forum will act as a vehicle for dialogue between young people and the association, and enable young people to represent themselves on the estate's tenants' association. The project also aims to establish the needs of young people in the community and to feed that information into the strategy for managing the estate. It has developed important partnerships with Camden youth service, which has provided support and youth work expertise.

Implications of welfare benefits and the New Deal for housing management

Housing management staff must be familiar with welfare benefits and the New Deal. They need to be aware of the impact that benefit sanctions, suspensions and disallowances and eligibility for the New Deal can have on their tenants. Social landlords need to be clear about their role and policies in relation to these issues. (See chapters 8 and 9.)

☐ Support

Young people need a range of support at different stages in their transition to independence. This support can be provided in a variety of ways, such as supported accommodation, floating support and supported lodgings.

Supported accommodation

Supported accommodation can provide a secure environment in which young people gain the confidence and skills to move on to independent accommodation. Local authorities and housing associations should develop partnerships with agencies that have the ethos, skills and expertise to develop the necessary provision.

Supported accommodation can be either shared or self-contained. Some young people benefit from sharing with others in similar circumstances, and learning valuable skills such as negotiation and compromise.

Edinvar Community Care Ltd supported accommodation

Edinvar Community Care Ltd runs the Slipway service, providing supported accommodation to vulnerable and homeless young people who have left care or have to leave home because of difficult family circumstances, and the SAILS service, providing supported accommodation to young people with mental health problems. Slipway and SAILS support 25 young people aged 16-20 in Edinvar's furnished accommodation and through visiting support to young people in their own homes. There is also a resource centre that the young people can use to meet other young people, do laundry, make meals together, and apply for jobs and training opportunities.

Support with both practical and emotional issues is provided on an individual or group basis, including a 24 hour on-call service.

→

Group and outdoor activities are organised, which enable young people to avoid being isolated, learn social skills in a safe setting and gain confidence by trying out new activities with adults they trust. Residents' involvement in running their support services includes participating in selecting staff, choosing the furnishings for their flat, selecting flatmates and planning and fundraising for group activities.

Authorities may wish to provide supported accommodation for young people while they are waiting for permanent accommodation after having been found homeless or accepted onto the housing register. This will help prevent those young people who have already approached the local authority falling back out of the system. Local authorities can also use their own general needs stock to provide a range of supported accommodation to young people, such as supported furnished scatter flats.

Organisations developing supported accommodation projects need to be aware of the precarious nature of funding for this sector. Project budgets that rely heavily on housing benefit should be reviewed in light of the interdepartmental review of housing benefit.

Glasgow City Council: supported scatter flats for young people

Single people are the largest applicant group for accommodation in Glasgow, accounting for 50 per cent of waiting list demand; 43 per cent of single waiting list applicants are under 25 years old. A five-tier youth homeless strategy has been developed consisting of:

- Mainstream housing suitable for young people, including some furnished flats
- Lightly supported furnished scatter flats — up to 30 in each of the 16 district housing offices
- Emergency furnished flats for young people over 18 who would otherwise be accommodated in adult hostels
- Short-stay, emergency-access hostel accommodation
- Medium-stay, planned-entry hostels

Scatter flats are mostly one or two-apartment housing in areas of medium demand. They are let initially on a temporary missive, and the service charge includes an element for support services. After approximately six months, or once support is no longer required, the tenant can remain in the flat on a permanent tenancy agreement with a reduced service charge.

Floating support

'Floating support' is an arrangement whereby tenants are given their own permanent accommodation with visits from a support worker. The level of support varies with the tenant's current requirements. When they reach a stage where they no longer require it, the support can be moved on to another tenant who does.

This arrangement is particularly appropriate for young people who are going through a transitional period in their lives, when they need to experience the minimum number of unnecessary disruptions and changes, such as moves between accommodation. Floating support is also particularly suitable when young people are widely dispersed and cannot access central support services.

There are numerous models of floating support. There may be a consortium of landlords who have a management agreement with one support provider. Alternatively, the support provider may also be the landlord. The exact nature of the relationship will be determined by the support being offered, the relative expertise of the agencies involved, and financial and legal requirements.

Funding arrangements for floating support can be complex. It is important to focus on the funding of the additional service. The cost of basic housing management and services provided for all tenants should be separated out so that when the support moves on to another tenant there is no confusion about charges.

The majority of floating support schemes for housing association tenants are eligible for special funding: SHMG from the Housing Corporation, SHRG from Tai Cymru, SNAP from Scottish Homes or SNMA from the DoE (NI). If a scheme involves a consortium of housing associations, or one association providing the support services for other associations' tenants, it is important to be clear which association will claim and therefore be accountable for the grant.

Other agencies are also in a position to fund floating support and many floating support services receive funding from:

- Local housing authorities: Revenue funding can be found by re-prioritising existing services that currently receive grant funding. The housing revenue account can be used to provide floating support to local authority tenants if the support is ancillary to the authority's landlord functions
- Social services departments: Social services can use a variety of approaches, such as grant aid to voluntary organisations, social services grant aid from local budgets and spot purchasing. Schemes should not rely entirely on spot contracting, since this makes it difficult to ensure continuity in

provision. Social services departments can also use their duties under the Children Act to fund floating support schemes for care leavers

- Probation: The probation accommodation grant scheme can be used to purchase floating support schemes
- Health authority
- Joint finance
- Specific grants: for example, mental illness and AIDS-specific grants
- Charitable funding

If the tenants being supported occupy stock developed with special needs capital funding above the general needs grant level, linked to revenue funding, housing associations face an issue of accountability. As the support is moved on, the tenant therefore becomes a general needs tenant. However, the property they are living in is still a special needs-funded property. In such instances, associations should discuss the position with the Housing Corporation, Tai Cymru, Scottish Homes or NIHE. If an association has received revenue-only funding to provide support to tenants in general needs stock, this situation will not arise.

With any supported housing scheme it is crucial that all the parties involved are aware of their responsibilities and the nature of the relationship between them. Clarity about roles and responsibilities is fundamental to the success of any scheme. Tenants will need to know who does what, while staff will need to know how and where their responsibilities interact with other workers, and who is ultimately responsible. Clear job descriptions and systems for management and supervision are a prerequisite.

Floating support checklist

- A clearly-defined scheme, with identified clients and a sufficient pool of properties
- Secure funding and awareness of associated accountability
- Clear service agreements between purchasers and providers based on activities and output
- Agreements between landlord and service provider
- Dedicated floating support management
- Tenant selection and assessment procedures
- Risk assessment procedures
- Procedures for reducing and withdrawing support, replacing properties and allocating individual tenants

- Progression strategies for tenants
- Equal opportunities, tenant involvement and participation, confidentiality
- Monitoring and review

Westminster: A partnership scheme providing floating support to care leavers

Centrepoint provides a floating support scheme for ten care leavers at any one time in Westminster. The scheme involves five partner agencies — Centrepoint, social services, housing, Peabody Trust and Network Housing Association. Care leavers are referred to the scheme from the social services' leaving-care team and given housing association tenancies. They are initially given an assured shorthold tenancy which becomes an assured tenancy when the floating support is withdrawn. Support is provided for an average of six months, but this can be extended.

Key Ring: A floating support project for people with learning difficulties

Key Ring has provided accommodation and support to people with mild or moderate learning difficulties since 1990. The service was developed in response to user demand. There are now 15 networks, each of nine people, around London and Surrey. Approximately one-fifth of the people supported are aged under 25 and a large proportion were previously homeless.

Tenants are given a local authority or housing association tenancy within walking distance of the eight other people in their network. They receive support from the other tenants and from a part-time community worker living in his or her own flat. The contract between the individual tenants and Key Ring includes the requirement to offer neighbourly support to one another.

Referrals are primarily from social services, which provides community care block contracts for each network. Each network costs approximately £25,000 per annum. The service has proved very successful, with an extremely low turnover of both tenants and staff. Housing providers have reported that Key Ring tenants have lower rent arrears and require less housing management intervention than other tenants.

Supported lodgings

Supported lodgings schemes involve a network of people who offer a room in their home, with varying levels of support, to young people. The scheme matches providers and lodgers and actively participates in the agreement between them (Button, 1994). Supported lodgings schemes do not offer direct access or take emergency referrals, unlike Nightstop (see above); they provide the informal support of a household and are not appropriate for people who need more intensive support. They are often initiated by social services departments. However, funding has been severely threatened by changes to housing benefit.

Many of the issues relevant to Nightstop schemes also apply to supported lodgings schemes, such as personal liability insurance, recruiting and training providers, police checks and referral agencies. The following factors must also be considered:

- Licences and agreements
- Complaints procedures
- Matching providers and lodgers
- Monitoring and supporting the placements
- Policies for dealing with placement breakdown
- Move-on arrangements

Albert Kennedy Trust: A supported lodgings scheme for young lesbians and gay men

The Albert Kennedy Trust provides temporary accommodation for young lesbians and gay men who are homeless or at risk of becoming so because their parents will not accept their sexuality. It works with social services to make appropriate foster placements for young people aged under 16; supported lodgings are arranged for those aged over 16. All of the Trust's accommodation is provided in the homes of approved 'big brothers' or 'big sisters', older gay men and lesbians who are secure in their own lives and sexuality.

Young people can either contact the Trust direct or be referred by another agency. A placement worker arranges a meeting with the young person to assess their needs, and the teenager is then introduced to the carers. A set of aims and objectives are decided at the beginning of the placement — such as getting a job, making more friends and learning to be independent. The young person and carers get to know each other over an introduction period of three or four weeks, after which they decide whether or not they want the placement to go ahead. Placement meetings take place every three months.

Starter packs

Local authorities are empowered to give grants to young people leaving care (see chapter 6). In certain circumstances young people may also be able to receive a community care grant. However, many young people will not have the resources to purchase the basic essentials to set up their own home. Where flexible options such as semi-furnished or furnished accommodation are not available, agencies have often provided young people moving into permanent accommodation with 'starter packs' of basic furniture and household goods. The cost of these packs is low and is often funded by charitable sources or churches. Local authorities may wish to provide funding for start-up and running costs of such schemes.

Support workers preparing young people for the move to independent accommodation should help them to develop realistic expectations, and make them aware of second-hand and inexpensive options. See chapter 9 for details of furniture stores projects.

South Herefordshire District Council starter packs for young people

In January 1996, South Herefordshire District Council allocated two rooms in its homeless person's hostel to the Young Single Homeless Project to provide temporary accommodation for young people. Many young people lacked essential household items or the means to purchase them when they moved on from the hostel, so a basic pack was provided including bedding, pots and pans, cutlery, crockery and a kettle. There is now a list of items from which young people can choose what they need. Local churches also provide £20 food vouchers that can be redeemed at local stores in the area.

☐ Conclusion and checklist

Providing young people with appropriate accommodation and support is central to enabling them to make the transition to independence and develop full lives. This accommodation and support will be provided by a wide range of organisations with a multiplicity of skills and expertise. The accommodation will be from all tenures. This variety will be reflected in an assortment of funding sources and reflects the diversity of young people who will use it. However, quality standards should be assured across the full range of provision.

When addressing housing management and support:

- Ensure that there is a range of appropriate accommodation available for young people as established by a needs assessment.

- If there is insufficient or inappropriate direct-access provision in the area consider developing a Nightstop/stopover scheme.

- Ensure that use is made of the private rented sector. Develop a landlord register, accreditation scheme and landlords' forum.

- Consider which is the most appropriate form of occupancy agreement for 16 and 17-year-olds. Do not discriminate against 16 and 17-year-olds in the provision of accommodation.

- Establish a procedure for assessing whether independent accommodation is appropriate for individual young people.

- Proactively manage young people. Consider appointing a young people's tenant support worker with a youth work background.

- Ensure that young people are actively involved in tenant participation.

- Ensure housing management staff are familiar with the implications of welfare benefits and the New Deal.

- Ensure there is a sufficient range of supported accommodation. Consider letting furnished local authority properties with support.

- Consider developing floating support services, particularly in rural areas.

- Consider developing a supported lodgings scheme. Ensure that such a scheme is sufficiently funded.

- Provide or fund starter packs for young people without the basic essentials for setting up home when they move into independent accommodation.

CHAPTER 8

Affordability

☐ Introduction

Ensuring that young people have a safe place to live is not just about providing them with accommodation; it is also about ensuring that they can afford it. As David Donnison (1980) said, "Most housing problems are really problems of unemployment, poverty and inequality."

This chapter considers rent levels; young people's benefit entitlements; who pays accommodation costs; and exemptions from single-room rent restrictions. It also discusses improving young people's access to the private rented sector through rent deposit/guarantee schemes; access to housing benefit and the interaction between Jobseeker's Allowance and housing benefit; and ways to increase young people's residual income.

It seems likely seems that housing benefit will be a major focus of the Government's Comprehensive Spending Review and this may result in significant changes to benefit entitlements.

☐ Rent levels

Neither housing associations nor local authorities are able to charge differential core rents for the same property. However, social landlords should ensure that rent levels are affordable for young people.

Rent levels must also be a major consideration in developing new provision. The Housing Corporation's 'Influencing Rents' policy (1996) restricts rent increases to changes in the retail price index plus one per cent. Rent levels are currently taken into account in the bidding process for general needs housing, and in the

1998/99 bidding round rent levels were requested for supported housing, although no benchmarks were used. Tai Cymru uses benchmark rents, and includes supported housing rents in calculating an association's overall average rent; this must be at or below the benchmark rent to secure capital funding. Scottish Homes requires associations to submit bids which include rent levels in line with its own rent policy, while the Northern Ireland Housing Executive expects associations' rents to be affordable.

Irrespective of these processes, local authorities should look carefully at rent levels when deciding which bids to support. Although local authority and most housing association tenants are not subject to the same benefit restrictions as private sector tenants, tenants will be subject to the same steep taper as benefit is withdrawn and so experience the same 'poverty trap'. This is particularly relevant for young people given their low average earnings (see box).

Box 8a: Young people's earnings, 1995

Average weekly earnings
Under 18

- Men £113.10 (31 per cent of average male earnings)
- Women £117.10 (44 per cent of average female earnings)

Aged 18-20

- Men £176.90 (48 per cent of average male earnings)
- Women £154.20 (58 per cent of average female earnings)

Aged 21-24

- Men £246.80 (69 per cent of average male earnings)
- Women £210.30 (79 per cent of average female earnings)

Source: *New Earnings Survey*, HMSO, 1995

☐ Young people's benefits

This section outlines the main benefits to which young people are entitled. For more detailed information refer to References and further reading.

Box 8b: Jobseeker's Allowance

Jobseeker's allowance (JSA) is a benefit for people who are unemployed, or work less than 16 hours a week, and are looking for full-time work. It was introduced in October 1996 to replace unemployment benefit and income support for people required to look for work.

There are two forms of JSA: contribution-based JSA, which replaced unemployment benefit; and income-based JSA, which replaced income support for unemployed people. The vast majority of young people covered by this guide will not be entitled to contribution-based JSA. The following information, therefore, is specific to income-based JSA (although some of it will also be the same for contribution-based JSA).

Entitlement
(Jobseekers Act 1995, sections 1-3) To qualify for JSA a person must:

- be unemployed or working (on average) for less than 16 hours a week; and
- satisfy the 'labour market conditions' i.e.
    - (i)   be available for work; and
    - (ii) be available for employment; and
    - (iii) be actively seeking employment; and
    - (iv) have a current jobseeker's agreement with the Employment Service; and
- be below pensionable age; and
- not be younger than 19 and still at school or college; and
- be in Great Britain, normally; and
- pass the means test.

The 16-hour rule
Students over the age of 19 are entitled to claim JSA if they receive 16 guided learning hours or less per week, and fulfil the other conditions detailed above. Part-time students are required to be available for and actively seeking work, and have a valid jobseeker's agreement.

Sanctions
(Jobseekers Act 1995, section 19) A JSA claimant can be sanctioned if, without 'good cause', they:

- fail to carry out a reasonable jobseeker's direction; or
- lost their job for misconduct; or
- leave a job voluntarily; or

➜

- fail to apply for a job notified to them by the Employment Service; or
- neglect to avail themselves of a reasonable opportunity of a job; or
- leave or give up a place on a compulsory training scheme or employment programme; or
- fail to attend a compulsory training scheme or employment programme on which they have a place; or
- neglect to avail themselves of a reasonable opportunity of a place on a training scheme or employment programme; or
- do not apply for a place on a compulsory training scheme or employment programme which has been recommended by the Employment Service or turn down the offer of such a training place; or
- lose a place on a compulsory training scheme or employment programme because of misconduct.

The sanction period varies according to the reason for the sanction and is either a fixed period of two or four weeks, or a variable amount between one and 26 weeks. During the sanction period no JSA will be paid, unless the person is entitled to a hardship payment. Although the payment of JSA ceases, the underlying entitlement remains and so all passported benefits, such as housing benefit, remain in place.

Suspension and disallowance
If a question arises about a claimant's entitlement to benefit, JSA will be suspended. This is most likely to be caused by concern that the claimant is not fulfilling the 'labour market conditions' — for example, if the claimant is not considered to be actively seeking work. An adjudication officer will then investigate and decide whether the claim should be disallowed. During the period of suspension, JSA should continue to be paid, unless the suspension happens at the beginning of the claim, in which case payment is not started.

JSA hardship payments
Hardship payments can be made if a person is likely to suffer hardship if JSA is not paid and:

- a person has claimed JSA and is awaiting a decision; or
- a person does not qualify for JSA because they do not satisfy the labour market conditions; or
- a person's benefit is suspended; or
- a person has been sanctioned.

Source: CPAG, *Jobseeker's Allowance Handbook*, 1997

Box 8c: Benefits for 16 and 17-year-olds

The benefit entitlements of 16 and 17-year-olds are a complex area. This box outlines the main benefits they may be entitled to. It is important to refer to more detailed benefit handbooks for further information (see References and further reading).

Income Support
Young people aged 16-17 can claim income support if they are in any of the following circumstances:

- Unable to work or go on a training course (IS (Gen) (JSA) Regs 1996 Sch 1B)

- On a training course and in receipt of a training allowance that is lower than their income support entitlement (IS (Gen) (JSA) Regs Schedule IB, para 28)

- In relevant education and in one of a number of categories (IS (Gen) (JSA) Regs Sch 1B, para 15); including those who are of necessity living away from their parents or any person acting in place of their parents because:
  - they are in physical or moral danger, or
  - they are estranged from their parents or any persons acting in their place, or
  - there is a serious risk to their physical or mental health; and including those who have been in local authority care and of necessity are living away from their parents or any person acting in place of their parents

- If they are sick (IS (Gen) (JSA) Regs 1996 Sch 1B, para 7)

Jobseeker's Allowance
Young people aged 16-17 are entitled to claim JSA if they fall into one of the following categories:

- Those eligible to claim JSA during the child benefit extension period (JSA Regs, reg 57), including those who are living away from parents or any persons acting in place of their parents because:
  - they are estranged from them, or
  - they are in physical or moral danger, or
  - there is serious risk to their physical or mental health

- Those who have just left custody or local authority accommodation are entitled to JSA for a limited time (JSA Regs, reg 60)

- Certain groups who are eligible to claim income-based JSA at any time (JSA Regs, reg 61)

→

- If they have little or no money and severe hardship would result unless JSA is paid (Jobseekers Act 1995, Section 16(1)). Severe hardship is not defined in the regulations. However, the following are considered:
  - accommodation, and the risk of losing any accommodation if JSA were not paid;
  - means of support, including any income or savings, and anyone else who could provide support;
  - health and vulnerability

Child Benefit
Child Benefit is only payable to parents. Likewise the child benefit extension period is only relevant for young people living with their parents.

Source: *Youthaid, Training and Benefits for Young People, 1997*

☐ Payment of accommodation costs

If a young person has a liability to pay either rent (for a tenancy) or a fee (for a licence), whether or not this liability is legally binding, they are eligible to claim housing benefit. (Section 130(1) of the Social Security Contributions and Benefits Act 1992.)

Box 8d: Housing Benefit

Housing benefit is paid to people who have a low income and pay a fee (whether rent or a licence fee) for accommodation. It is paid whether or not the claimant is available for or in full-time work. A person can claim housing benefit if the following conditions are satisfied (Social Security Contributions and Benefits Act 1992, section 130):

- His/her income is low enough
- His/her savings and other capital are not worth more than £16,000
- S/he or his/her partner is liable, or treated as liable, to pay rent for accommodation. It does not matter if s/he is in arrears, or if s/he has paid his/her rent in advance
- S/he normally occupies that accommodation as his/her home, or is only temporarily absent from it
- S/he does not fall into one of the groups of people who are treated as not liable for rent even if s/he has to pay rent, or the payments they make are not eligible rent for housing benefit.

→

People treated as not liable for rent include:

- Full-time students, with a few exceptions
- 'Persons from abroad'
- Those who pay rent to someone they live with and either it is not a commercial arrangement, or s/he is a close relative
- Those who have made an arrangement to pay rent in order to take advantage of the housing benefit scheme
- Those who became jointly liable to pay rent within eight weeks of having been a non-dependant of one of the other joint occupiers, unless s/he can satisfy the local authority that the change in arrangements was not made to take advantage of the housing benefit scheme
- Those who are a member of, or are fully maintained by, a religious order
- Those who are living in a residential care or nursing home

Local reference rent (LRR)
Local reference rent was introduced for new private rented sector claims in January 1996, as part of a new formula for calculating the maximum amount of housing benefit payable. It is defined as the midpoint of reasonable market rents for assured tenancies of an appropriate size. New claims for housing benefit are now restricted by reference to the LRR (Regulation 11 of the Housing Benefit (General) Regulations 1987 as amended).

Single room rent (SRR)
Since 7 October 1996, single people under the age of 25 living in the private rented sector have had their housing benefit entitlement limited to the 'single room rent' (Circular HB/CTB A11/96).

SRR "represents the general [i.e. average] level of local rents for a single room without board and attendance but with a shared use of toilet and either the shared use of a kitchen or no kitchen at all" (paragraph 4A(A) of Schedule 1 of the Rent Officers (Additional Functions) Order 1995). Local authorities have the discretion to pay above the limit in cases of 'exceptional hardship' subject to an overall cash limit set by the Department of Social Security.

This change affected all new and change-of-address claims for housing benefit made on or after 7 October 1996, and claims following a break in entitlement of four weeks or more. It also affects existing claims from the first review date on or after 7 October 1997.

→

A number of groups of people are exempt from these restrictions:

- Married and cohabiting couples
- People with care of children
- People exempt from the changes to housing benefit introduced in January 1996.

See Box 8f for additional exemptions.

Source: CPAG (1997) *National Welfare Benefits Handbook*

☐ Implications of the Children Act 1989

If a social services department fulfills its duty to provide accommodation under Section 20 of the Children Act 1989, it is liable for rent payments and cannot pass these on to the young person. DSS Circular HB/CTB A16/96 states that a young person is not liable for the cost of accommodation which the social services department is "providing as part of an ongoing duty". This applies regardless of the type of accommodation, whether the duty arises out of a care order or other section of the Act, who owns the accommodation, and whether the child has entered into an agreement for the provision of accommodation.

So, while a young person is being accommodated as part of an ongoing duty of the social services department under Section 20 of the Children Act 1989, social services are liable to pay for the cost of that accommodation and the young person is not entitled to claim housing benefit. Once that duty has ceased, however, the young person is liable to pay any charges and can therefore claim housing benefit.

There are long term implications for the level of housing benefit a young person is entitled to, depending on which section of the Children Act 1989 they are assisted under. If social services discharge their duty under section 20 of the Children Act 1989, the young person will be exempt from single room rent restrictions until the age of 22. If social services discharge their duty under section 17, the young person will be subject to single room rent restrictions, except where a care order was in place after the age of 16. (See Chapter 5 for more detail on the Children Act.)

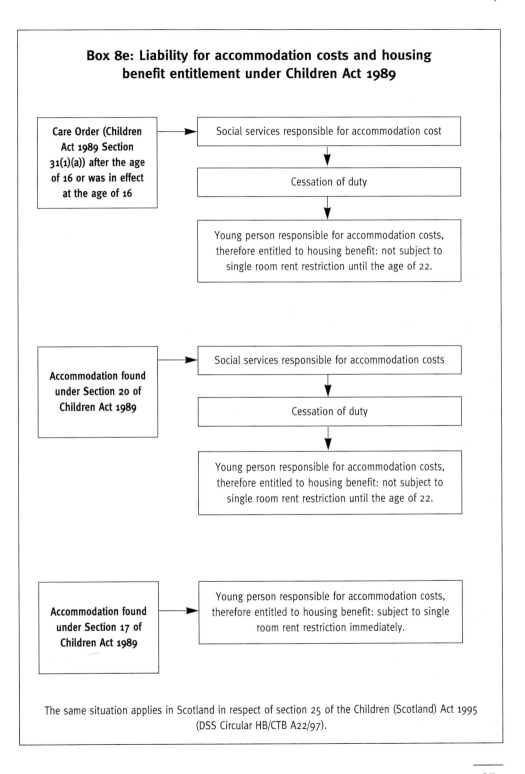

Box 8f: Exemptions from single room rent restrictions

Those exempted from single room rent restrictions include any person:

- whose landlord is a registered housing association

- who is under 22 years old and was previously subject to a care order under section 31 (1) (a) of the Children Act 1989 made either after he was 16, or before he was 16 and remained in force after he reached that age

- who is under 22 years old and was previously accommodated under section 20 of the Children Act 1989 (Note: the young person does not have to have been housed in local authority owned or run property; they only need to have been provided with their accommodation by the local authority under this section of the act)

- who is under 22 years old and was previously subject to a supervision requirement by a children's hearing under section 44 of the Social Work (Scotland) Act 1968 made in respect of him which continued after he had reached 16. However, this exemption does not apply where the sole ground for supervision was the need for care specified in section 32 (2) (g) of the Act (commission of offences by child); or the supervision requirement meant that he had to reside with a parent, guardian, friend or relative

- who is under 22 years old and for whom parental rights were previously vested with the local authority by a resolution under Section 16 of the 1968 Act made in respect of him which continued after he reached 16

- who is under 22 years old and was previously in the care of a local authority under section 15 of the 1968 Act after he had reached 16

Source: *Housing Benefit and Council Tax Circular A5/97*

☐ Rent-in-advance and rent guarantee schemes

The majority of young people seeking accommodation use the private rented sector. However, their access is severely restricted by the need to pay a deposit and rent in advance. This problem can be overcome by rent deposit and rent-in-advance schemes. It may also be appropriate for support to be provided in conjunction with these schemes; this section should therefore be read in conjunction with chapter 7.

Impact of housing benefit changes

Single room rent restrictions have clearly had an impact on young people's access to the private rented sector and landlords' attitudes towards them (Griffiths, 1997). It is crucial that this is taken into account when developing a scheme.

It is also important to consider providing deposits or guarantees for accommodation where the rent is above the local reference rent or single room rent. Housing benefit restrictions must be explained to young person.

Developing a scheme

Developing a rent-in-advance or rent deposit scheme involves:

- **Establishing local need:** How long are young people staying in short-term hostels and projects? What is the experience of letting agencies trying to secure accommodation for young people? What is the experience of young people? What are landlords asking for? (See chapter 3 for more detail on assessing needs.)

- **Establishing a planning group:** This group will oversee the development process and may manage a project once it is up and running. It should have good representation from relevant agencies or carry out detailed consultation.

- **Agreeing aims and objectives:** What is the group hoping to achieve by setting up a scheme? Objectives will need to be specific.

- **Establishing landlords' needs:** For a scheme to be successful it is necessary to identify the key factors stopping landlords from letting to young people. The range of services that can be offered to landlords include the following:
  - support and advice
  - training
  - an assurance that housing benefit applications will be completed and the landlord kept up to date with the progress of the claim
  - prior assessment of potential tenants
  - support provided to tenants
  - standard tenancy agreements and inventories
  - rapid replacement when a tenant leaves
  - rent in advance
  - rent deposit
  - damage and theft guarantees
  - rent arrears guarantee
  - assistance in dealing with disputes

- **Selecting and supporting tenants:** A scheme will need to establish criteria for selecting suitable tenants. It may also be appropriate to provide support in addition to the deposit or guarantee. Link workers may be employed, on a paid or voluntary basis, to support young people in their properties and assist with finding accommodation (see below), negotiating rent and housing benefit applications.

- **Selecting and vetting properties:** Will the scheme be using self-contained or shared properties, or both? Will properties be identified via letting agencies or through direct contact with landlords? Does the local authority operate a registration scheme for houses in multiple occupation? Will it be possible to vet properties that the tenant has identified?

- **Vetting landlords:** Will the scheme vet landlords, or will it make it clear to tenants that it accepts no liability for landlords' behaviour? What procedures are in place if it becomes apparent that a certain landlord is not appropriate: will existing tenants be advised to move?

- **Monitoring and evaluation:** It is important to establish appropriate monitoring and evaluation systems. These systems may need to evolve to include different or additional information.

Ipswich Rent Deposit/Guarantee Scheme

The Ipswich Rent Deposit/Guarantee Scheme, for single people for whom no agency has a statutory duty, is administered by Shaftesbury Homes. It assists clients by finding accommodation, negotiating rent levels, vetting landlords, providing housing benefit application support, and conducting initial and final inventories. It provides the landlord with full rent in advance until housing benefit is received and guarantees against any losses. The scheme is funded by Ipswich Concerned Churches.

Further information on rent/deposit guarantee schemes is shown in Box 8g on page 101.

Housing benefit recipient

Someone claiming housing benefit can ask for it to be paid direct to their landlord or to a body acting on the claimant's behalf. The decision will be made by considering a number of factors:

- How much control does the project wish to retain?

- How large is the fund and how will losing money affect the scheme?

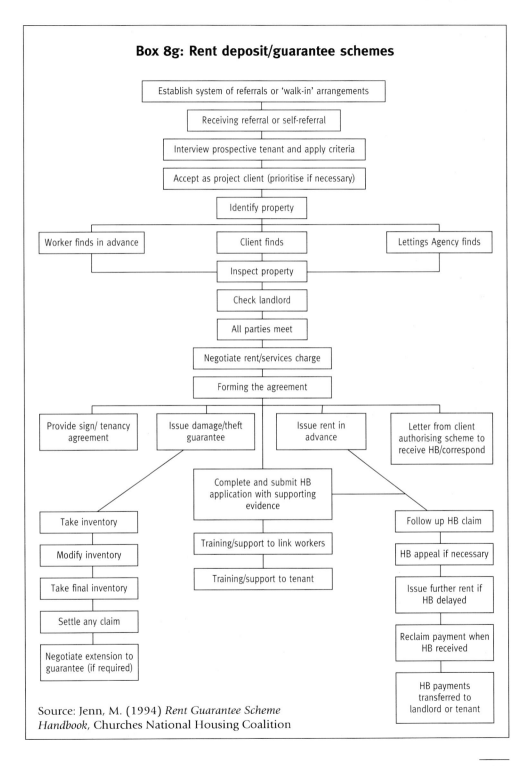

Box 8g: Rent deposit/guarantee schemes

Establish system of referrals or 'walk-in' arrangements

Receiving referral or self-referral

Interview prospective tenant and apply criteria

Accept as project client (prioritise if necessary)

Identify property

Worker finds in advance — Client finds — Lettings Agency finds

Inspect property

Check landlord

All parties meet

Negotiate rent/services charge

Forming the agreement

Provide sign/ tenancy agreement — Issue damage/theft guarantee — Issue rent in advance — Letter from client authorising scheme to receive HB/correspond

Complete and submit HB application with supporting evidence

Take inventory — Training/support to link workers — Follow up HB claim

Modify inventory — Training/support to tenant — HB appeal if necessary

Take final inventory — Issue further rent if HB delayed

Settle any claim — Reclaim payment when HB received

Negotiate extension to guarantee (if required) — HB payments transferred to landlord or tenant

Source: Jenn, M. (1994) *Rent Guarantee Scheme Handbook*, Churches National Housing Coalition

- Is the scheme giving money or a guarantee to the landlord? A guarantee is usually preferable.
- How much responsibility should the tenants have?
- What impact will direct payment to the landlord or scheme have on the tenant's self-confidence and budgeting skills?
- What are the landlord's requirements?
- What effect will direct payment to the landlord have on, for example, the speed at which repairs are carried out?

Even if housing benefit is to be paid directly to the landlord, interim arrangements may need to be set up if payment is delayed. The scheme may guarantee payment to the landlord by a certain time whether or not housing benefit has been paid.

Colchester Borough Council: A rent deposit scheme that guarantees payment to the landlord by a specified date

The local authority operates this scheme for anyone who is homeless but not in priority need. Landlords receive two services. They are guaranteed the first three weeks of 'eligible rent' by the seventh week of the person's stay, irrespective of whether or not housing benefit is eventually paid; and a six-month, extendable deposit covering a loss of up to £120 arising from damage or theft. This guarantee can be extended for a further six months if necessary.

Funding

Rent-in-advance and rent deposit/guarantee schemes are relatively inexpensive to run. A certain amount of capital is required to set the project up. There will also be costs for administration and any support services (see chapter 7). However, the actual fund will not need to be particularly large. If the scheme offers guarantees to landlords, payments will only be necessary when housing benefit is delayed or if any property is damaged or stolen. If the scheme hands money over to the landlord for deposits or rent in advance, a slightly larger pool of money may be required, but it should be replenished as housing benefit is paid and as tenants move on. However, retrieving deposits can add a significant administrative burden.

Funding for schemes can come from a wide variety of sources, including churches, charitable trusts and the local authority. The DETR has provided section 180 funding for the administration costs of a significant number of these schemes.

It is important to consider whether young people will be required to repay any money paid out on their behalf. This may add additional administrative costs. There are also implications for the young person's ability to budget, and to take independent responsibility for themselves. A condition of joining the scheme may be that the young person is required to save money to cover the value of the deposit or guarantee. This would ensure that the fund is not depleted too quickly. It would also have the effect of enabling young people to move on to other private sector properties without assistance in future.

Wintercomfort rent deposit scheme

The agency Wintercomfort's Rent Deposit and Support Scheme (RDSS) is aimed at people who are homeless and/or in temporary accommodation. RDSS provides rent up front, deposit guarantees and support to enable people on benefits or low incomes to set up home in the private sector. There are currently four schemes running — for Cambridge City, South Cambridgeshire, East Cambridgeshire and Uttlesford.

Referral criteria include the ability to hold a tenancy and manage independent accommodation, plus at least three months' residency in the local area. Extra support is provided by volunteer 'link workers' who work with the tenant and landlord to ensure that the tenancy runs smoothly. People on the scheme are encouraged to save a small amount of money every week, so that they will be in a position to put up the deposit themselves when the time comes for their tenancy to be run independently.

Money or guarantee

It will be necessary to decide whether to offer landlords a guarantee of payment up to a certain value, or to pay them directly and claim it back later. This decision will be based on a number of factors, including:

- **Landlords' wishes:** If the scheme has already established a relationship, landlords may be willing to trade advance payment against the knowledge that the young people referred to them will have been selected according to agreed criteria and will receive a degree of support.

- **Administrative arrangements:** Will it be more costly regularly to have to recoup money paid out or to negotiate individual payments when the need arises?

- **Housing benefit recipients:** If the scheme is giving the landlord the rent in advance, is it appropriate for the scheme to receive any housing benefit?

☐ Access to housing benefit

Landlords are often unwilling to take claimants because housing benefit is paid slowly and, since 7 October 1996, four weeks in arrears. Improving housing benefit administration will help improve young people's access to the private rented sector.

Interim payments

Local authorities are required to deal with housing benefit claims and to pay benefit within 14 days insofar as possible (Regulation 88(3) HB Regulations). If the authority has been unable to assess a private sector tenant's claim within 14 days, the tenant should receive a payment on account while the claim is being dealt with (Regulation 91(1)). The tenant does not have to ask for this payment to be made; it should be made automatically. These interim payments are not discretionary. They can only be refused if it is clear that the claimant will not be entitled to housing benefit, or if the reason for the delay is that the claimant has been asked to provide evidence and has failed to do so without good cause. If the delay has been caused by a third party — for example, a bank or employer — the obligation to make an interim payment is not affected (CPAG, 1997, *National Welfare Benefits Handbook*, page 274).

Fast tracking benefit applications

In addition to interim payments, housing benefit offices should also consider fast tracking applications for young people in the private rented sector. Swift, regular payments will reassure landlords who are often unwilling to let to young people, and will enable young people to budget more successfully. Housing benefit offices may wish to consider assigning responsibility for young people to a specific officer, as is the case with the Benefits Agency.

Camden Council: Confirmation of housing benefit claims

Camden housing benefit department has a boarders' section, primarily for non-priority need homeless people who are seeking accommodation in hotels and bed and breakfast hostels. Claimants are provided with a letter for their landlord confirming that a claim has been made. Because of the good reputation of Camden's benefits division, hotel owners accept this letter as sufficient and allow the claimant to move in.

Regular contact between landlords and housing benefit offices will also establish relationships and procedures that will affect young people's access to the private rented sector. Voluntary agencies, too, may wish to cultivate relationships with both housing benefit offices and the Benefits Agency. This will enable agencies to resolve difficulties and develop good practice.

Bridges One Door, Edinburgh: Strong links with the Benefits Agency

The Benefits Agency in Edinburgh is working with Bridges One Door to pilot a good practice model in offering a more casework-oriented approach to young people. This is in addition to well-established quarterly meetings between itself, Bridges One Door and the Citizens Advice Bureau. These address difficulties on a city-wide basis and promote a quality service and more consistent standard of practice for homeless young people. Bridges One Door also attends the bi-monthly multi-agency Consumers' Liaison Council organised by the Benefits Agency.

Short-term hostels

Hostels can experience significant difficulties in claiming housing benefit for short-stay residents. The following options should be considered for improving benefit administration and collection:

- Night-by-night payment in conjunction with a nightly licence agreement
- A retrospective claiming procedure with the local housing benefit office, only claiming once the young person has left the hostel
- Collecting all supporting evidence for each claim before the young person leaves the hostel

---

Westminster City Council: Nightly payment of housing benefit

Centrepoint's Berwick Street hostel has established a system of night-by-night retrospective housing benefit claims with Westminster City Council. Young people can stay at the Berwick Street hostel for up to two weeks under a nightly licence agreement. Every Sunday, Centrepoint faxes the housing benefit office with a list of names, signatures and date of first night for all young people who have moved into the hostel that week. During their first week in the hostel each young person completes a full housing benefit form, which is sent on to the benefit office after they leave. The claim is then processed retrospectively and the hostel paid for the number of nights that the claimant stayed.

Impact of Jobseeker's Allowance sanctions, suspensions and disallowance

It is very important to be aware of the impact of benefit sanctions, suspensions and disallowances, both on young people's continued entitlement to housing benefit and their ability to pay service charges. This section should be read in conjunction with Box 8b.

If a young person is subject to sanctions they will not be paid Jobseeker's Allowance for a specified period, although they may be entitled to apply for a hardship payment. They retain their underlying entitlement to JSA, however — and, therefore, to passported benefits such as housing benefit — so there should be no need for a young person to make a revised claim for housing benefit.

If a young person's JSA is suspended pending a decision regarding their entitlement, entitlement to passported benefits cease. In this situation it is necessary that the young person makes a fresh housing benefit claim.

It is essential, therefore, that a young person is aware of whether they are subject to a sanction or suspension. Benefits Agency staff and housing workers must explain the importance of making a new claim for housing benefit if JSA has been suspended or disallowed.

In many housing projects young people will be paying for some services out of their JSA. If their benefit ceases, this will clearly affect their ability to pay those charges. Housing managers need to be clear about how they will deal with such situations. It will be important that young people are supported in making hardship payment claims. In addition housing managers will need to decide whether they will:

- continue to expect regular payment, and operate the standard eviction procedures if young people fail to pay;
- roll forward service charges until payment can be re-started, at which point the young person will be expected to pay off arrears; or
- suspend service charges for the period during which benefit is not paid, with the project carrying the cost.

Housing benefit extended payments

Claimants who have been on income-based JSA or income support for six months are entitled to continue to receive housing benefit for four weeks if they start working 16 or more hours per week or lose JSA or income support through increased part-time earnings. The job must last at least five weeks and claims must be made within eight days of coming off JSA or income support (CPAG, 1997, page 250).

☐ Grants to residents on low income

The steep withdrawal of housing benefit a young person experiences as they enter employment makes it extremely difficult for them to make the transition from welfare to work. Ineligibility for housing benefit also makes it extremely difficult for young people to sustain full-time study. It is not possible for housing organisations to charge differential rents, but they can provide financial support for young people making the transition from benefit to employment, education or training.

Charitable rebate schemes

Agencies can provide a discretionary grant to young people who are in low paid employment, education or training. Schemes of this type need to establish eligibility criteria, and whether to award a flat-rate payment or a variable amount increasing young people's income to a set rate. These grants could be funded from charitable sources.

Centrepoint grants to residents on low income

Centrepoint provides a charitable rebate scheme for residents in low-paid employment or studying full-time. The scheme is funded by the Bankers Trust and administered by project managers. Initially there was a sliding scale of grants to ensure that residents only paid 25 per cent of their income in rent. Demand has increased, however, and eligible residents are now given a flat rate grant of £10 per week for up to one year.

The scheme is designed to encourage residents to take up education or work opportunities. Residents are eligible, therefore, if, after joining Centrepoint, they enter higher education or work with a wage of less than £150 per week. The scheme is particularly aimed at young people who missed out on education and need pre-vocational training.

☐ Conclusion and checklist

Affordability is one of the main factors restricting young people's access to suitable housing. Although agencies have to work within restrictions governing the level of rent they can charge and the amount of benefit young people are entitled to, there are significant steps they can take to ensure that young people receive their full entitlement. Innovative approaches can assist young people to make the transition to work, education or training and therefore to financial independence.

- **Rent levels:** Ensure that rent levels are affordable both for existing stock and future developments. Consider rent levels carefully when applying for funding or supporting funding bids. Bear in mind that young people's income is likely to be below average.

- **Benefit entitlement:** Ensure staff are familiar with basic information on young people's benefit entitlements. Establish links with a local advice agency for more detailed information when needed.

- **Accommodation costs:** Establish which agency is responsible for a young person's accommodation costs. Is it housing benefit or social services? Check whether a young person is exempt from the single room rent restrictions.

- **Rent deposit/guarantee schemes:** Establish or support a rent deposit scheme. This will require careful planning. Who will receive the housing benefit? How will the scheme be funded? Will money payments or a guarantee be used? How do single room rent restrictions affect the scheme?

- **Access to housing benefit:** Ensure housing benefit offices are making some payment to private sector tenants within 14 days of claims. Establish relationships with Benefits Agency and housing benefit offices. Ensure swift payment, particularly to young people in private sector accommodation. Negotiate nightly retrospective payment for short stay hostels.

- **Impact of JSA sanctions, suspensions and disallowances:** Ensure housing benefit payment does not cease as a result of JSA sanctioning. Ensure straightforward information is provided to young people regarding their JSA claims and whether they need to make fresh claims. Ensure young people make fresh claims for housing benefit when appropriate. Decide how service charges will be treated if a young person's benefit is withheld for a period of time.

- **Residents on low income:** Establish a rebate scheme to assist young people in the transition from benefit to work, training or education.

CHAPTER 9

Skills and Training

☐ Introduction

This chapter outlines government training programmes aimed at 16 and 17-year-olds. The New Deal for young people aged 18-24 is discussed in detail, including ways for agencies to become involved in delivering it. The New Deal has the potential to build on many programmes already working with homeless and marginalised young people. These include estate-based initiatives, training for the housing industry, and foyer schemes, which have successfully promoted a holistic approach to young people's housing and training needs. Other 'New Deals' — such as for older or disabled people — are not dealt with here.

☐ Government employment and training programmes for 16 and 17-year-olds

Apart from the New Deal, which is discussed below, many other initiatives are targeted at young people. Unlike the New Deal, these often cover 16 and 17-year-olds.

Modern Apprenticeships

Modern Apprenticeships are designed to enable more young people to achieve higher level qualifications, including NVQs at level 3. They are mainly for 16 and 17-year-olds but other young people are also eligible if they can complete their training before the age of 25. There are no educational qualifications needed for entry but most Modern Apprentices are recruited as employees and employers set their own requirements. Modern Apprenticeships have been developed in 75 industrial, commercial and service sectors by national training organisations in partnership with Training and Enterprise Councils (TECs) and employers with government support and funding. These include non-traditional areas such as estate agency and childcare, as well as the more traditional craft areas in engineering and construction. Just over 164,000 young people have started on the initiative since its launch in 1995.

Investing in Young People

Investing in Young People is a major government education and training programme. Like the Target 2000 programme, which it replaces, it includes the National Traineeships, New Start and Right to Study schemes.

National traineeships: These were introduced in late 1997 as one of the measures to replace Youth Training. They are designed very much along the lines of Modern Apprenticeships with the focus on NVQs and key skills at level 2. Eligibility is as described above for Modern Apprenticeships. They are available in 28 industrial, commercial and service sectors, with training frameworks currently being developed in about 40 more.

New Start: New Start, introduced in England in September 1997, is designed to bring back into learning those young people who for various reasons have either dropped out, or are at risk of dropping out, of education, training and employment. Local partnership projects are being funded to build on and draw together existing initiatives.

Right to time off for study or training: The government is introducing legislation to ensure that all 16 and 17-year-olds in a job will be entitled to paid time for study or training to pursue appropriate qualifications.

☐ The New Deal

The New Deal explained

The New Deal is designed to give employment, education and training or work-related experience to all 18 to 24-year-olds who have been registered unemployed for six months or more. It was introduced in 'Pathfinder' areas in January 1998 and across the country in April 1998. Some £3.5 billion has been committed to the New Deal over the period 1998-2002, with 70 per cent of those funds targeted at young people aged 18-24.

The New Deal consists of three stages, each of which is discussed in detail later:

- The Gateway
- The Options
- The Follow Through

Implementation of the New Deal has been devolved to regional and district Employment Service offices, with local partnerships responsible for delivery. It is important to ensure that the local partnership addresses the needs of particular client groups.

Eligibility for the New Deal

All 18 to 24-year-olds will automatically enter the 'Gateway' after they have been claiming Jobseekers' Allowance (JSA) for six months. In addition, some young people can choose to enter the Gateway at an earlier stage. These include:

- Those who are in special needs groups: people with disabilities; returners to the labour market; ex-regulars in HM Forces; ex-offenders; lone parents; people whose first language is not English, Welsh or Gaelic; those with reading, writing or numeracy problems; and those who have become unemployed as the result of large-scale redundancies

- Those who have left local authority care in the last three years

- Those who would already have been required to enter the Gateway but for short breaks from claiming JSA totalling no more than 28 days

In addition, the Employment Service is able to exercise discretion in favour of early access for 18 to 24-year-old JSA claimants who, in the opinion of an Employment Service New Deal personal adviser, are at a particularly severe disadvantage in their search for work as a result of problems such as homelessness or drug dependency.

It is important that agencies working with homeless young people or those at risk of homelessness form links with the Employment Service and encourage early access for suitable young people. Existing multi-agency forums must include a representative of the Employment Service and agencies should jointly develop protocols for referring homeless young people to the Employment Service for early access.

Young people who come within the New Deal client group will be helped to decide which of the options is most suitable for them, and assisted in securing specific places. During the Gateway period, appropriate places will be identified for those who continue to claim JSA, if they have not already selected one. All young people will receive written notification of the place they are required to take up. If they do not take it up — or they leave it early — they will be referred to independent adjudication. Unless they can show good cause, they will lose two weeks' JSA. Any further refusal will result in the loss of four weeks' JSA. People in vulnerable groups — for example, those who have children, who are pregnant or who have significant caring responsibilities — will be able to claim JSA at a reduced rate if they can show that they would otherwise suffer hardship.

Manchester: Joint working between the Careers Service and the housing department to provide homeless young people with employment guidance

In 1996, the funding partnership between Manchester Housing, Careers Partnership, the local TEC and Hulme Regeneration made a successful bid to the European Social Fund (Objective 3) and seconded a careers officer to work directly with the young single homeless team in the housing department. This team provides temporary accommodation for single homeless young people and a comprehensive resettlement package and support when they are rehoused.

The careers officer built up a caseload made up solely of people living in temporary accommodation secured by the team. New links between training agencies and employers helped this group gain access to education, training and work. The officer acted as an advocate on behalf of young people with employers and also offered one-to-one sessions to build confidence and help them to write cv's.

The Gateway — assessment of housing need

As a young person enters the Gateway period, which lasts for up to four months, they are allocated a personal adviser, who will remain their contact point throughout the programme. Gateways will differ across the country, but they will all have access to specialist support and must provide:

- An initial phase of help to find unsubsidised jobs — this is particularly relevant for those who are able to take work without additional help
- Advice and guidance about finding work
- Access to independent careers advice and guidance
- For those who need it, access to a range of measures to improve immediate job prospects
- If appropriate, help to prepare for a suitable New Deal option
- In the case of people with exceptional problems (for example, homelessness, drug dependency or debt), help from specialist agencies
- For young people who would particularly benefit, access to a mentor who would provide advice and encouragement on a voluntary non-'official' basis
- An action plan, which participants will retain during the New Deal and which will be updated when necessary
- Referral to New Deal Options

It is important that the Gateway stage includes a proper assessment of housing needs. Employment Service staff will not be in a position to assist young people in finding appropriate accommodation. Housing agencies will need to work closely with the Employment Service and/or the Gateway contractors, therefore, with clear agreement about the role of local authority housing and social services departments.

Black young people are nearly three times as likely to be unemployed as white young people, and some groups within the black community have been hit even harder by high levels of unemployment and lack of training opportunities (Chauhan, 1997). Approximately 13 per cent of 18 to 24-year-olds who have been unemployed for more than six months are black, whereas only 8 per cent of the working population in that age group is black (Simmonds et al, 1997). Agencies involved in delivering the New Deal must therefore be able to demonstrate a track record of high quality work with the black community.

The Options

It is estimated that 40 per cent of the young people who enter the Gateway will get unsubsidised work without additional help within the four month period. The remaining 60 per cent will have access to up to four options.

- **The employment option:** Private, public and voluntary sector employers are offered £60 per week to provide employment for six months on a standard wage. The employer has to show that the job does not replace an existing one. The young person must undertake one day's training per week, for which a further £750 will be paid to the provider. It will also be possible for young people to pursue self-employment as part of the New Deal.

- **The full-time education option:** This allows young people without an NVQ level 2 (or equivalent) qualification to attend an approved course for 12 months without losing their benefit entitlement. Discretionary travel and similar grants may be available.

- **The voluntary sector option:** Young people receive their benefit plus a grant of £400, paid weekly or fortnightly over six months, to work in the voluntary sector. The placements must include one day's training per week, for which a further £750 will be paid to the provider. The provider also receives a contribution towards the cost of facilitating the placement. The placement must be designed to benefit the local community.

- **The environmental task force option:** Young people receive their benefit plus a grant of £400, paid weekly or fortnightly over six months. Again, they must receive one day's training per week. The work must fall into a number of categories of local, regional or global environmental action and sustainable development.

Organisations that want to become involved in the New Deal do not have to be able to deliver all of it. In many areas, consortia are likely to take on large parts of the New Deal from the Employment Service and subcontract tasks out. The local authority may be best placed to take on the main contract and then subcontract out to the voluntary sector.

'Benefit plus' or a wage?

Under the environmental task force and voluntary sector options providers can opt to pay participants a wage, as opposed to young people being on 'benefit plus'. Employers can set their own wage levels, and will receive a government subsidy equivalent to the 'benefit plus'. It is important to bear in mind that if a young person becomes an employee they lose passported benefits such as free prescriptions and free dental treatment.

The Follow Through

The government is keen to avoid the 'revolving door' syndrome of previous training initiatives. The 'Follow Through' is recognition that not all young people will secure employment and that, having invested in someone for 10 months, it is important not to drop that responsibility. The young person's adviser will remain with them until they find a sustainable employment outcome.

Organisations should carefully consider whether they have the skills and resources to deliver the Follow Through. They must not assume that if they are able to deliver the Gateway they are automatically able to deliver the Follow Through.

Housing organisations as New Deal providers

Housing organisations are well placed to become directly involved in the New Deal, particularly as providers of the Gateway or the employer or environmental task force options. Many foyer schemes are already carrying out elements of the Gateway, and there are many other examples of local labour and training programmes running alongside development activity and routine maintenance work. Organisations should discuss what they can offer with their local Employment Service office, and decide where this fits best with the New Deal.

There are a number of issues that organisations need to consider when deciding whether to offer New Deal placements:

- **Quality assurance:** It is crucial that the placements offered to young people under the New Deal are high quality. Key indicators should be established and regularly reviewed.

- **Training:** Considerable emphasis has been placed on the quality of training young people should receive under the New Deal. Because housing organisations are unlikely to be able to offer this element, they will need to link up with reputable training providers. It will be important to monitor the quality of the training offered, its suitability for the young person and the placement they are in and the effect it will have on their employability.

- **Progression strategies:** Under the employer option, participants take up jobs that are expected to be permanent. This may not always be possible, so employers need to develop a progression strategy. They should be aware of the range of available options and assist young people in finding alternatives.

NomadPlus: A programme providing personal development and skills training to recently resettled young people

The Sheffield NomadPlus programme is designed to provide personal development and skills training to enable young people to remain in their own homes and to access mainstream opportunities. The programme provides a city-wide service for people aged 18-25 who have been homeless and have just been offered housing.

Each programme runs over three months, catering for ten people at a time. The activities take place over six half-day sessions each week:

- Half day in base group for general group support
- Half day supervised use of resources room (including IT) with tuition
- One day at the Nomad furniture project or other placement
- Half day following up own interests or other placement
- Half day in organised training session.

Participants are also provided with access to the resource room at other times, one hour per week with a personal mentor, travel expenses and stationery. The first young people to use the programme were closely involved in developing the project: for example, choosing IT resources, designing project leaflets and evaluating how the project responds to their needs. Initial feedback indicates that they particularly valued having a place to talk about their experiences with other people in a similar position.

Implications of the New Deal for housing staff

Social landlords are likely to have tenants who will be eligible for the New Deal. They need to decide how they will respond to it, and should:

- Survey tenants, or use existing statistics, to establish how many are aged 18-24, whether they receive JSA and whether they come within groups that can enter the Gateway prior to six months.

- Make sure services continue to be accessible and appropriate. Day centres or advice services may have to consider opening in the evenings or at weekends. Review fixed hostel meal times or curfews for people working shifts or unsociable hours.

- Develop close working relationships with the Employment Service. Agencies should demonstrate how they can assist in delivering the New Deal, establish protocols for referring young people for early entry to the Gateway, enable a thorough assessment of housing need during the Gateway and advise on appropriate additional support.

- Clarify the role of housing management staff. As agents of a young person's landlord, are they able to act as New Deal mentors or would this result in a conflict of interests? To what extent will housing managers 'police' young tenants' involvement in the New Deal, particularly in light of the impact of non-cooperation and loss of JSA? If the organisation is providing one of the options, will that affect the landlord-tenant relationship?

- Provide tenants and users with information about the New Deal.

- Pay particular attention to 16 and 17-year-olds, who are not eligible for the New Deal.

- If young people choose to move to find work, or move having secured employment, they will need to find accommodation. Local housing authorities should not include a period of residency in their criteria for access to the housing register. Such restrictions are illegal in Scotland.

☐ Employment training programmes

Basic principles

There are a huge variety of employment training programmes on offer. Many have been specifically developed for working with young people in housing need.

London Connection: A core skills pack designed specifically for use with homeless young people

London Connection provides a range of services to homeless and unemployed young people, including a core skills pack developed specifically for use with homeless young people and funded by the Employment Service. The pack offers the following features:

- A fully accredited training programme, including opportunities to achieve the NCVQ standards for core skills at levels 1 and 2

- 150 hours of training materials, arranged in 16 separate modules, addressing three main themes: employment and training, housing and self-reliance

- Training materials based on the experience of homeless young people and issues confronting them

- Information on designing, delivering and evaluating courses using the materials contained in the pack

- A modular structure that can be used to construct programmes ranging from one-day workshops to one-year part-time courses

Source: London Connection, 1995

Although employment training uses widely varying styles and formats there are some basic principles:

- All programmes should assess trainees individually and be tailored to meet their specific needs.

- Employers should be involved.

- Training courses should validate young people's skills and experience. This does not have to involve accreditation. Examples of skills on a cv may be as valid as having an NVQ. With young people who are homeless or in housing need, 'soft' indicators such as continued attendance may be as appropriate as 'hard' indicators such as getting a job.

- Training provision should not be funding-led.

- The environment should be appropriate for young people.

- Training provision should be flexible, allowing young people to work on appropriate tasks and not follow a programme in a fixed order. Young people should be allowed to re-enter training programmes as many times as is necessary.

- Young people should be prepared for the 'flexible labour market'. Training programmes should not raise unrealistic expectations. Young people are likely to have to move between jobs on short term contracts, possibly interspersed with periods of unemployment. Employment training should equip them to deal with this.

Types of training

Employment training programmes should offer a comprehensive menu of services, from core skills training through to assistance in accessing individual job opportunities. Clearly, training should meet the needs of the young people it is aimed at, but agencies can decide to focus on one type of provision or a range of options:

- **Core skills:** Numeracy, literacy, communication skills, self-confidence. This training can be delivered in a variety of ways, not necessarily in a traditional classroom.

- **Job search skills:** Writing cv's, filling in application forms, writing business letters, telephone skills, interview skills, information technology.

- **Vocational training:** Gaining skills for specific jobs.

- **Working with employers:** Mentoring, mock interviews, work placements, work shadowing. Contact with local employers can provide invaluable experience. Familiarity with interview procedures and the work environment can significantly improve young people's chances of getting work, particularly if they have had no previous contact with people in work. Mentoring programmes can also be useful, but agencies need to be closely involved in these from the start.

PRESET: Mentoring for young people from ethnic minorities

Presentation Education and Employment Charitable Trust (PRESET) aims to provide opportunities for disadvantaged young people, particularly those from ethnic minorities, living in inner cities, to fulfil their educational potential and assist them into sustainable employment. This is achieved through a **bursary scheme**, under which PRESET sponsors young people to continue in education or to enter training schemes; and a **mentoring programme**. This is designed to provide positive role models who can offer guidance and support, and raise confidence and self esteem.

Streets Ahead recruitment agency for homeless people

Streets Ahead recruitment agency is based in Holborn, central London. It works with anyone who has been affected by homelessness within the previous two years and who is 'job ready', motivated and wanting to work. Jobs can be found in four main industries: administration and secretarial support, information technology, retail and catering.

Although companies are charged a fee to use Streets Ahead, the agency is client-led, not employer-led. Clients are only sent to employers when they are ready for the job; if they are not successful Streets Ahead will continue to seek an appropriate employer. Clients who are not suitable for the agency are referred to another organisation — for further training, for example, or job preparation.

Streets Ahead is staffed by three recruitment consultants and an administrator; all staff have a recruitment background. Since opening it has developed a job preparation consultant post and an IT centre with a trainer providing flexible individual training. Streets Ahead also has a large clothing bank of smart, good quality suits and formal clothes that can be used for interviews. In its first year of operation it registered 355 people, of whom over 100 were found work.

☐ Employment training and the housing industry

The main issues to be considered in providing employment training for young people are the same in the housing industry as elsewhere:

- The quality of placement — young people should be given real work
- The quality of training — does the organisation have the skills to provide this or should it be contracted out?
- The payment of a wage or 'benefit plus'
- Progression strategies for the organisation and young people
- Possibilities for re-entering the programme

Training placements should never substitute for existing jobs.

Building work

With the release of capital receipts there is now more scope for local authorities and housing associations to train young people in the construction industry. This need not be restricted to site-based trades. Social housing providers should develop a good relationship with contractors and local trainers to ensure that young people receive appropriate, high-quality training and support.

Employment training can also form part of a Single Regeneration Budget, Estate Action or Estate Renewal Challenge Fund programme, or part of an Urban Programme in priority partnership areas in Scotland. Local authority housing departments can act as the lead agency for such a programme, drawing in agencies with expertise in training. Trainees will appreciate the fact that they are taking in part in real work rather than a 'make-work' training programme, and that it is of clear value to the local community. They can also take advantage of training opportunities in a wide variety of skills and professions.

Lewisham Community Refurbishment Scheme

Lewisham Community Refurbishment Scheme was set up in 1993 by the housing department to work with its estate action programme to revitalise four deprived housing estates in Deptford. It is a two year scheme offering training in bricklaying, carpentry, electrical installation, plumbing, and painting and decorating; and providing trainees with on-site experience to build up their working speed and contacts within the building industry.

The performance of the scheme is measured against five main target indicators:

- 85 per cent attendance in the first month of each intake
- 75 per cent of those left after the first month should complete the scheme
- All trainees should get 48 weeks on-site training
- 80 per cent of those who finish the scheme should gain a NVQ level 2
- 50 per cent should enter paid employment within two months of finishing the scheme

Trainees attend Lewisham college on a day or block release basis to gain a NVQ level 2 in their trade. They receive benefit plus £10 for the first six months, rising to £200 per week for the last six months. They also receive protective clothing, basic tools, a travel allowance, 18 days paid holiday per year and literacy and numeracy support throughout the scheme if necessary. The scheme also offers childcare provision of up to £75 per child per week with council-registered childminders or a council nursery.

Portsmouth Housing Association: A 'local labour in construction' scheme

In 1994, Portsmouth Housing Association, working in partnership with Warden Housing Association, Barratt Homes and Ideal Homes Southern, set up and ran a local labour scheme to redevelop the Rowner estate near Gosport.

The high levels of unemployment in the area made a 'local labour in construction' scheme a priority. As a condition of the building contracts, therefore, it was agreed that 25 per cent of the labour was to be provided by Gosport residents, with priority being given to residents of the Rowner estate. Local job centres set up a register of construction skills and actively marketed people on the list to the contractors and subcontractors working on the site. Local training providers were also involved.

The scheme did have problems with customised training and finding ways for youth trainees, who required a two-year commitment from an employer, to be taken on by highly mobile subcontractors. Overall, however, the Rowner scheme was successful in recruiting local people and experience of it led private housebuilders to overcome their initial lack of enthusiasm. By the six-month stage, contractors had exceeded the 25 per cent target, employing 103 local people. The scheme also demonstrated that it is possible to meet most costs for such a project from normal development expenditure, rather than revenue subsidies.

Housing management

Training in housing management provides young people with a wide range of skills that are applicable to a variety of professions. Many college courses arrange placements for students, and there is a requirement to undertake an element of practical work to gain a Chartered Institute of Housing recognised qualification.

PATH Local Authorities: Providing housing management training for black people

PATH Local Authorities (PATH LA) was jointly established by the Federation of Black Housing Organisations and the Chartered Institute of Housing to provide training for black people to undertake housing management duties in local authority housing departments and housing associations.

→

PATH LA provides a work and training programme made up of three elements. First, work experience placements are arranged so that each placement builds on the skills and knowledge gained in the preceding placement. Second, the trainee is provided with two supervisors, one from the placement and one from PATH LA, who monitor progress and ensure that s/he continues to benefit from the programme. And third, each trainee undertakes a college course on a day-release basis. In most cases the course chosen will also lead to a recognised housing qualification. Specialist short training courses are also provided to address areas of skill and knowledge.

The intermediate labour market

The intermediate labour market concept is based on the belief that there are many things that need to be done in local communities that have economic value and improve the quality of life; and that even if conventional training programmes can raise the employability of the long term unemployed, there is a shortage of jobs and so they cannot all be re-employed. The intermediate labour market gives long-term unemployed people a route back to work and increased self-esteem by providing skills training, counselling, motivation, work experience and a living wage while working on socially-useful projects in a commercial environment. Paying a wage rather than 'benefit plus' is critical.

Wise Group, Glasgow: Development of an intermediate labour market

The Wise Group started life in 1983 as a Scottish Neighbourhood Energy Action project in Glasgow. (SNEA is a voluntary organisation established to tackle problems of cold, damp housing.) The first project, Heatwise, was funded by Glasgow District Council and developed under the Manpower Services Commission's Community Programme. Since that time the Wise Group has expanded significantly. Funding comes from a wide variety of sources including Local Enterprise Companies, Training and Enterprise Councils, the European Commission, local authorities and earned income.

The Wise Group aims not only to provide people with training and employment, but also to make a positive impact on the community. One of the group's specific aims is to raise the purchasing power of low-income households and improve residents' quality of life. This has been achieved by reducing householders' fuel bills through energy advice and efficiency measures; making homes more secure; whole-house refurbishment; and improving the external environment in some of the most deprived areas of Glasgow.

→

The Wise Group's clients are predominantly young and male, and disproportionately long-term unemployed. Trainees gain qualifications and an increased likelihood of finding employment after the programme.

Self build

Self-build projects provide young people with skills and training in construction, project management, financial control, negotiation and dealing with contractors — and, of course, somewhere to live. They also give young people self-esteem and confidence and an ability to operate successfully as part of a group. Self build should not be seen as a solution to immediate housing problems, but as a way of developing a young person's skills and experience. Self-build projects require careful planning and preparation and a significant investment in time and resources. The young people will need continued support and guidance throughout the process.

There are a variety of approaches to self-build projects and to the level of involvement in the building process. Young people may contract out part or most of the work, or they may train and work alongside qualified professionals, becoming qualified and experienced themselves.

Frontline Self-Build Project, Leeds

Frontline Self-Build Housing Association was set up in 1987 by 12 unemployed Afro-Caribbean people from the Chapeltown area of Leeds. Frontline had four main aims:

- to gain training and qualifications in specific aspects of the building trade;
- to use the skills gained during training to build homes for each member of the project;
- to transfer skills gained throughout the period of training and practical work into other building fields; and
- to provide positive role models and a pilot for other groups in Leeds.

The local authority offered a site on a deferred purchase basis and funding was obtained for an 18-month coordinator's post to liaise between the professional contractors and the self-build association. Frontline established a shared ownership option with Leeds Federated Housing Association, with funding from the Housing Corporation and private finance. It also negotiated with Leeds TEC to secure training places with Henry Boot contractors, who seconded a foreman to the project with charitable funding.

Furniture provision

Many agencies have developed furniture store projects, collecting unwanted household items, which are then supplied to people who have recently got their own tenancy and/or are on low income. Often these items need repairing and, in the case of electrical goods, testing. Some projects work with young people as trainees to restore and repair these items.

Valleys Furniture Recycling

Valleys Furniture Recycling is a limited company with charitable status. Donated furniture is collected from people in Rhondda Cynon Taff. Items are checked and if necessary repaired before being displayed in their showrooms. Furniture is then delivered to people on benefit or low incomes. A small donation is suggested for each item.

Volunteers are provided with tools and a safe working environment to enable them to practise existing skills. Unskilled volunteers learn from skilled workers. All volunteers receive training in health and safety and customer care. Training is also provided in IT and use of electrical testing equipment. Volunteers receive formal recognition of their involvement and the project provides prospective employers with references. A quarter of volunteers leave for full-time paid employment.

☐ Foyer schemes

Foyer schemes combine accommodation with access to training and employment, providing an integrated approach to young people's housing and employment needs. Many foyers also have a commercial space that supports the project financially and may offer training and employment opportunities to young people.

Box 9a: Foyer Federation for Youth definition of a foyer

The Foyer Federation has adopted three criteria that define a foyer scheme:
- The focus is on helping disadvantaged young people aged 16-25, who are homeless or in housing need, achieve the transition from dependence to independence.
- It is based on a holistic approach to young people's needs, offering integrated access to, at a minimum, accommodation, training and job-searching facilities.

→

- The relationship with a young person is based on a dynamic formal agreement as to how the foyer's facilities and local community resources will be used by that person in making the transition to independence, commitment to which is a condition of continuing residence in the foyer.

Source: Foyer Federation for Youth, Newsletter Spring 1997

Foyer provision varies widely. It need not even be all on one site. In rural areas, a dispersed foyer may link accommodation spread across an area to employment training facilities in a central location. This type of arrangement can often make use of existing stock. Depending on staffing levels, foyers can accommodate young people with a range of support needs, although they will not be appropriate for young people with very high needs.

If a foyer is to be developed, it should be as part of a strategic planning process, which will also establish what sort of foyer is most appropriate (see chapter 2). The specific issues that arise include:

- **Funding:** Putting together a capital and revenue funding package for foyers is notoriously difficult. It needs to cover all the elements of the foyer — accommodation, support, employment training and commercial space — and so is likely to come from a wide range of sources.

- **Occupancy agreement:** Agencies need to decide whether the requirement to undertake some form of employment training should form part of a young person's occupancy agreement, and consider the effects of young people losing their accommodation due to not having fulfilled their training obligations.

- **Training provision:** Is the training function provided in-house or is it contracted out? If it is contracted out, what control does the accommodation provider have? What is the day-to-day relationship between the staff? How do young people receive a consistent message?

- **Staffing:** Will the same staff provide housing management and support and employment training? Do staff have the skills to deliver the two functions? Is it appropriate for an agent of the landlord to provide assistance in looking for employment and training? If different staff groups provide the two services, what are the links between them? What information do they share about residents? Are they managed by the same person?

- **Move-on arrangements:** As with any form of non-permanent accommodation, planning should include move-on arrangements. In order to cater for individual needs, the length of stay should be flexible, and there should be a range of move-on options, including nomination agreements with the local authority and housing associations.

Foyers may wish to be involved in delivering the New Deal. They may be particularly well placed to provide aspects of the Gateway. However, it should not be assumed that they can deliver this service; and the implications — particularly for staffing levels — should be carefully considered.

Knightstone Housing Association foyer scheme

This Yeovil foyer scheme was developed by Knightstone Housing Association in partnership with other agencies. Knightstone established a post to work solely on the project. The local diocese donated a vacant church and construction training opportunities, leading to NVQs, were offered during its conversion. Funding sources included social housing grant, the National Lottery, charitable trusts, goods in kind, the local TEC and the European Social Fund.

The foyer provides 39 bedspaces, an IT suite, conference rooms and training facilities. It has established links with local employers, and also works with local young people who do not need somewhere to live but do require some assistance in seeking work. The NatWest Bank has recently funded a mediation and enterprise project. This is designed to prepare young people for flexible working patterns by exploring less traditional ways of working, such as cooperatives, self-employment, LETS (non-cash trading) schemes and volunteering.

In addition to a training worker, the foyer also employs a youth worker to develop initiatives that develop young people's self-confidence and networking skills. Young people were heavily involved in developing the foyer, being consulted about the design, ethos and policies. Local students designed a mural for the exterior walls, and local youth club users were on the staff interview panels. Residents now control part of the redecoration budget, and they are developing a formal residents' panel out of the current weekly meetings.

The foyer is part of a consortium that has bid to deliver the New Deal Gateway in the area.

Belfast foyer scheme

The first foyer in Northern Ireland, this opened in 1997 under the management of the Simon Community. It consists of 42 single-occupancy bedsits, common rooms, an employment training suite and a commercial restaurant space, which is let rent-free under a profit-sharing arrangement between Simon NI and the caterers. Each bedsit has an incoming telephone line enabling young people to give potential employers a personal number as opposed to the main foyer number.

☐ Conclusion and checklists

Young people do not simply need housing; they also need the means to be economically independent. The New Deal provides opportunities for agencies working with young people to take a fresh look at their housing, employment and support needs, and approach those needs in a holistic and coherent manner.

New Deal checklist

- Establish links with the Employment Service, possibly through existing multi-agency forums. Contact the local authority department that is leading on the New Deal in your area. Inform these bodies about the services different housing organisations in the area provide and how they might assist in delivering the New Deal.

- Establish protocols for referring homeless young people to the Employment Service for early access to the Gateway.

- Reach agreements with the Employment Service about how agencies can assist in meeting young people's housing needs during the Gateway and ensuring that housing need is a thoroughly assessed.

- Discuss with the Employment Service which part of the New Deal existing services best fit; find out who the main contractors are in the area and consider subcontracting; and ensure that the services being offered are what young people need rather than what is most likely to attract funding.

- Ensure that services continue to be appropriate and accessible in light of the New Deal — for example, opening times for day centres and advice services.

→

- Establish the number of tenants who are likely to be affected by the New Deal and monitor its impact.
- Clarify the relationship between housing management staff and tenants.
- Provide tenants with information about the New Deal, using newsletters and other forms of communication.
- Make sure that local authorities do not include a period of residency in the area as a requirement for access to the housing register.

Skills and training checklist

- Ensure that all staff working with young people have a basic knowledge of government training programmes.
- Ensure programmes are appropriate to young people's needs. Provide a range of training from core skills to specific jobs in conjunction with private sector employers. Ensure that young people have access to the clothing and equipment they need.
- Ensure that training for employment for local young people forms an integral part of a comprehensive approach to area regeneration.
- Consider all aspects of your work to establish whether it is possible to provide training opportunities for young people. Link up with agencies with expertise in providing training in those areas.
- Consider the need for self build and foyer projects during your strategic planning process, and provide a supportive environment for these projects.
- When developing a foyer consider the most appropriate model for your needs; involve young people in the development process; and make sure all elements have secure funding. Will the requirement to undertake some form of training form part of the occupancy agreement? Have move-on arrangements been made? Is it appropriate for the foyer to be involved in delivering the New Deal?

CHAPTER 10

Monitoring and Evaluation

☐ Introduction

Monitoring and evaluating services, policies, procedures and strategies is often undervalued or forgotten. In her survey on the implementation of the Children Act 1989, for example, McCluskey (1994) found that only 24 per cent of the responding local authorities were able to provide statistics on Children Act assessments.

It is essential to carry out monitoring and evaluation and to feed the results back into service development. Monitoring indicates which parts of the process are working, why they work and thus how services can be improved. It is an integral part of service delivery and strategy implementation and should be a continual process.

☐ Basic principles

There are a wide range of reasons for carrying out monitoring and evaluation, both internal and external, and proactive and reactive. These include:

- Meeting funders' and regulators' requirements
- Assessing service use
- Tailoring existing services
- Assessing need
- Developing new services
- Lobbying and campaigning

In his discussion of the Children Act, Brody (1997) says: "Both social services and housing departments should be monitoring the numbers of young people who come to them for assistance and the number who are provided with a service. Monitoring should also inform the process of needs assessment and planning. A full assessment of the needs of an individual ought not to be viewed as a snapshot process based on one interview. Rather, it might be part of a rolling process which monitors the progress of the young person and informs future planning and service provision. Monitoring needs to be made an integral part of the process of drawing up the Children's Services Plan."

Whittaker (1993) presents a strong case for mandatory and detailed ethnic monitoring: "Without it there will be a continuing denial of the size of ethnic communities, and a consequent inability of local authorities to take account of the diversity of cultures that exist within their areas." This is already acknowledged by the Department of Health which states that "it [ethnic monitoring] should be carried out routinely [by local authorities] and translated into policy, service design and practice, which in turn should be monitored."

Clarity about the purpose of monitoring will help to determine what information is collected. Monitoring systems must be designed to ensure that this information is both relevant and sufficient, and that it is possible to explain the relevance and use of each item of information to staff and young people.

As frontline staff usually have the responsibility for collecting basic monitoring information it is essential to explain to them the purpose of the exercise and to provide training. This will improve return rates. Similarly it is good practice to explain to young people why information about them is being collected and how it will be used. This can either be done verbally or with a written explanation on monitoring forms, along the lines of: "This information will help us to ensure that the service we provide to you and other young people is appropriate to your needs. Information about the people who use this service also enables us to secure funding to help us stay open. Your identity will never be disclosed in any reports or information based on this monitoring."

☐ **Monitoring individual services**

Each agency should monitor the use of its services. Monitoring should not simply provide a profile of service users, but should also record the outcome for each young person. Standard 17 of First Key's *Standards in Leaving Care* (1996) covers service monitoring and evaluation for care leavers (see Box 10a). The principles outlined in this standard are applicable to other services.

Box 10a: First Key's Standards in Leaving Care — Standard 17

Those agencies providing services to care leavers have systems in place for the monitoring of services and for the evaluation of outcomes for these young people. The findings of these systems are utilised in future service design and development.

(a) A system of evaluation which measures outcomes for young people against specified targets (in housing, education, employment etc) is in place and this is monitored by the senior designated officer.

(b) Evaluation incorporates the views of, and feedback from, the young people.

(c) The results of such an evaluation are reported on a regular basis to the appropriate levels of management.

(d) The results of such an evaluation are considered at regular intervals by the appropriate inter-departmental/inter-agency structures.

(e) The results of such an evaluation are incorporated into service design so as to ensure necessary improvements in service.

Source: First Key, *Standards in leaving care*, 1996

Piloting a monitoring system

When introducing a new monitoring system it is important to pilot it first, in order to:

- Remove ambiguous questions and ensure all questions are comprehensible.

- Remove repetitive and unnecessary questions.

- Ensure questions give the information required. For example, the question "Where are you moving on to?" may produce answers such as "Peterborough", whereas the information required is the tenure that residents are moving into. In this instance a question with tick-box options is preferable to an open question.

- Avoid the cost and inconvenience of implementing one monitoring system and then discovering that it needs replacing.

Agencies with a number of services

If one agency has a number of projects, it may be necessary for different projects to have different monitoring systems appropriate to their particular client groups. But even when using different monitoring systems it is beneficial to have a core set of information that is collected across projects (see below for more discussion). Where it is feasible to collect additional information questions can be added on.

Monitoring and confidentiality

Monitoring systems must be properly linked into confidentiality policies. Young people must be made aware of the ways in which any information will be used and the degree of confidentiality afforded. A disclaimer such as the following could appear on the questionnaire: "Your identity is confidential to the project, and you will never be identified personally in any reports or information based on this monitoring. We ask for your name, date of birth and gender in this sheet just so that we can compare the information in this questionnaire with details about when you leave the project. This top sheet will be separated from the rest of the form."

☐ Monitoring the local situation

It is also important to monitor the situation in the local area to gain a more representative picture of need.

Common monitoring systems

Agencies may choose to develop common monitoring systems that draw their information requirements together. This can become unwieldy, however, since different agencies are answerable to regulators with different requirements. It may be preferable, therefore, to establish a common base set of information, and then for each agency to tailor their monitoring system to meet their own needs and those of their regulators.

Information from joint initiatives can usefully feed into the local picture. For example, a vacant bedspace information service (see chapter 4) can be used to monitor the use of services.

Tracking young people's movements

If agencies coordinate monitoring systems it is possible to track young people's movements across accommodation and other services. This requires a unique identifier for each young person. An effective and confidential way of doing this is to use the young person's initial, date of birth and gender to produce a nine digit identifier like 'KF220979M'. Tracking individual young people's movements makes it possible to build up a picture — such as the extent to which individuals move from direct-access hostels to longer-term accommodation — and investigate any patterns which emerge. If, for example, a lot of young men are returning to short-stay projects, this may lead to an investigation of the provision of appropriate move-on accommodation for young men.

☐ Monitoring the local strategy

A local strategy must be monitored at a number of levels. The proposals for service development must be translated into a workplan with priorities, responsibilities, deadlines, targets and measures of how to identify success. The implementation of this workplan, as with any other, must be monitored and reviewed at regular intervals.

Best practice suggests that, as well as regular reviews, an independent evaluation should be commissioned at some stage. An independent body will be able to talk to all parties involved, including young people, and assess the implementation of the strategy. It will also establish the factors that were helpful and unhelpful in achieving its targets; this is particularly important because strategy development involves such a range of organisations.

The impact on young people locally must also be monitored. Information on the local situation, the level of need and the use of services can feed into this review process, which may eventually demonstrate the need to change parts of the strategy or its priorities. This must only be done following proper consultation.

Interpretation of information

Evaluating questionnaire results, analysing statistics and interpreting data is a complex task that should be carried out by skilled and trained staff, and is therefore only touched on here.

Most important, perhaps, is to bear in mind that a correlation between factors does not necessarily imply causation. In order to develop the appropriate response, a trend or tendency must not be automatically attributed to the most obvious factor; it requires proper investigation. For example, during 1996-97 Centrepoint saw a 13 per cent increase in the number of young people using its services who had slept rough at some stage previously. This could mean a number of things. It could mean that more young people were sleeping rough during that period, possibly as a result of changes to housing benefit from October 1996. Alternatively, it could be that more people with experience of sleeping rough were now using Centrepoint's services. Without further investigation it is impossible to give the reason for the increase.

Norfolk Social Services and Norwich Housing Services: A monitoring process that feeds into a six-monthly review of the joint protocol

The joint protocol for homeless young people in Norwich covers monitoring. Norwich Housing Services and Norfolk Social Services keep a record of each referral and its outcome. In addition, each agency completes a monthly monitoring form and sends it to Norfolk Social Services for analysis. The two bodies meet twice a year to review these arrangements and information on the operation of the protocol is published annually.

The monitoring form records the following information for each homeless young person:

- Date
- Name
- Sex
- Date of birth or age
- Referred from, including home area if not Norwich
- Referred to
- If no action, state why: young person refused/inappropriate request/other
- Indicate statutory response: Children Act assessment/Housing Act assessment/housing waiting list/not applicable
- Indicate outcome — immediate and subsequent: young person's rented home/accommodated by family or friends/accommodated by agency/no service arranged and why/not applicable.

In order to avoid double counting, agencies record information by name. However, each young person is assured that the information is collected for statistical purposes only, that no personal information will be published or released and that after collation the information is shredded.

☐ Conclusion and checklist

Monitoring and evaluation must form an integral part of a strategy for housing young people. In developing monitoring and evaluation systems, consider the following:

- Be clear about the reasons for carrying out monitoring and evaluation and therefore what information needs to be collected.

- Inform frontline staff and young people of the reasons for collecting the information, and provide training for staff.

- Pilot new or revised monitoring systems.

- It may be appropriate to use different approaches for different projects, but ensure that core information is collected for all projects.

- Ensure that the issue of confidentiality is addressed in the development and use of monitoring systems.

- Consider developing common monitoring systems with other agencies. It may be appropriate for only core information to be common to all of them.

- Consider developing tracking systems so that it is possible to monitor an individual's movements across provision.

- Ensure that the implementation of the local strategy is monitored. This should include an evaluation of the factors that helped and hindered the process. The impact and continuing relevance of the strategy should also be reviewed.

- Ensure that properly trained staff interpret the information collected. Do not mistake correlation for causation.

REFERENCES AND FURTHER READING

Chapter 2

Arnstein, S (1969) A ladder of citizen participation; *Journal of American Institutes of Planners*, Vol XXXV, No 4

Audit Commission (1992) *Developing local authority housing strategies*; HMSO

Department of the Environment (1995) *Housing Strategies — Guidance for local authorities on the preparation of housing strategies*

Evans, A (1996) *We don't choose to be homeless — Report of the national inquiry into preventing youth homelessness*; CHAR

Goss, S and Blackaby, R (1998) *Designing Local Housing Strategies: A Good Practice Guide*; Chartered Institute of Housing and Local Government Association

Malpass, P and Means, R (1993) *Implementing housing policy*; Open University Press

McCluskey, J (1997) *Where there's a will — A guide to developing single homelessness strategies*; CHAR

Watson, L & Conway, T (1995) *Homes for independent living — Housing and community care strategies, a good practice guide*; Chartered Institute of Housing

Chapter 3

Bramley, G (1989) *Meeting housing need*, a report on research for the Association of District Councils; ADC

Bryman, A (1988) *Quantity and quality in social research*; Unwin Hyman

Centre for Housing Policy (1997) *Young people and housing*; Rural Development Commission

Environment Select Committee, House of Commons Paper 22 — *Housing Need*, Session 1995/96

Housing Act 1985; HMSO

Housing (Scotland) Act 1987; HMSO

Kleinman, Morrrison and Whitehead (1994) 'Forecasting housing demand and housing need'. In *Development and planning*, edited by Cross and Whitehead; Newbury for Department of Land Economy, University of Cambridge

van Zijl, V (1993) *A guide to local housing needs assessment*; Institute of Housing

Watson, L and Harker, M (1993) *Community care planning: A model for housing needs assessment*; Institute of Housing and National Federation of Housing Associations

Welsh Housing Office Management Advisory Panel (1993) *Taking Stock: A guide to local housing assessment*

Whitehead, C and Kleinman, M (1992) *A review of housing needs assessment*; Housing Corporation

Williams, M et al (1995) *The Plymouth foyer: Views of young people*; Department of Applied Social Science, University of Plymouth

Chapter 4

Department of the Environment (1995) *Housing strategies: Guide for local authorities on the preparation of housing strategies*

Housing Corporation (1997) *ADP Bulletin 1997/98*

Chapter 5

Anderson, I & Morgan, J (1997) *Research report No 1, Social housing for single people? A study of local policy and practice*; Housing Policy and Practice Unit, University of Stirling

Asylum & Immigration Act 1996; HMSO

Brody, S (1996) *The Children Act and homeless 16 and 17-year-olds: A practical guide to assessment, accommodation and support*; CHAR

Children Act 1989; HMSO

Children (Northern Ireland) Order 1995; HMSO

Children (Scotland) Act 1995; HMSO

Code of Guidance on Homelessness (1997); The Scottish Office

Code of Guidance Parts VI & VII of the Housing Act 1996 (1996) — Allocation of housing accommodation, Homelessness; Department of the Environment, Department of Health

Code of Guidance Parts VI & VII of the Housing Act 1996 (Allocation of Local Authority Housing and Use of Nomination Rights, Homelessness Advisory Services, Homelessness) Welsh Office Circular 9/97 and amendments

Department of Health (1991) The Children Act 1989 Guidance and Regulations; HMSO

Homelessness (Persons Subject to Immigration Control) (Amendment) Order 1997 (SI1997/628)

The Homeless Persons (Priority Need) (Scotland) Order 1997 (SI1997/3049)

Housing Accommodation and Homelessness (Persons Subject to Immigration Control) Order 1996 (SI1996/1982)

Housing Act 1996; HMSO

Housing (Northern Ireland) Order 1988

Housing (Scotland) Act 1987

Thain, M (1996) *Homelessness and the Children (Scotland) Act 1995: Using the Children (Scotland) Act to help homeless people*; Shelter Scotland

Welsh Housing Quarterly (1997) *Exclusions from social housing*; WHQ Issue 28, 1997

Chapter 6

Biehal, N et al (1995) *Moving on: Young people and leaving care schemes*; HMSO

British Youth Council (1996) *Issues affecting young people: Being young in 1990s Britain*; leaflet

Centrepoint (1997) Annual statistics 1996/97

Children Act 1989

Children (Northern Ireland) Order 1995

Children (Scotland) Act 1995

Code of Guidance on Homelessness (1997); The Scottish Office

Code of Guidance Parts VI & VII of the Housing Act 1996 (1996) — Allocation of housing accommodation, Homelessness; Department of the Environment, Department of Health

Education Reform Act 1988

Evans, A (1996) *op cit.*

First Key (1996) *Standards in leaving care: Report of the national working group*

Housing Corporation (1994) *Fact file No 1*

Lee, P and Murie, A (1997) *Poverty, housing tenure and 'social exclusion'*, Findings, Housing research 222; Joseph Rowntree Foundation

Page, D (1993) *Building for Communities*; Joseph Rowntree Foundation

Chapter 7

Button, E (1994) *Supported lodgings: A good practice guide*; Centrepoint

Cameron, K (1997) *A foot in the door: A guide to good practice in developing and managing young people's direct access hostels*; Centrepoint

CVS Consultants (1997) Feasibility study on floating support in Hampshire

Gill, F and Mogollon, J (1996) 'Housing 16-17 year olds', *Sitra Bulletin*, July 1996; Sitra

Griffiths, S (1997) *Benefit shortfalls: the impact of housing benefit cuts on young single people*; Shelter

Housing Act 1985

Housing Act 1988

Housing Corporation (1996) Housing Corporation circular 05/96, Tenancies for people aged 16-17 years

Law of Property Act 1925

Luba, J & Fullwood, A (1996) A licence to occupy, *Housing* magazine, September 1996; Chartered Institute of Housing

Page, J (1992) *An Introduction to Nightstop*; National Nightstop

Power, A & Tunstall, R (1995) *Swimming Against the Tide*; Joseph Rowntree Foundation

Redmond, P and Stevens, I (1990) *General principles of English Law*; M&E Handbooks

Settled Land Act 1925

Spafford, J (1994) *Centrepoint Oxfordshire: A regional approach to a national problem*; Centrepoint

Welsh Federation of Housing Associations (1994) *Letting housing association homes to under 18-year-olds*

Chapter 8

CPAG (1997) *Jobseeker's Allowance Handbook* 1997/98

CPAG (1997) *National Welfare Benefits Handbook* 1997/98

DSS Circular HB/CTB A9/96

DSS Circular HB/CTB A16/96

DSS Circular HB/CTB A5/97

DSS Circular HB/CTB A22/97

Donnison, D (1980) 'A policy for housing', *New Society* Vol 54, No. 938

Griffiths, S (1997) *Benefit shortfalls: The impact of housing benefit cuts on young single people*; Shelter

HMSO (1995) New Earnings Survey

Housing Corporation (1996) *Influencing rents*

Jenn, M (1994) *Rent guarantee scheme handbook: Housing homeless people in the private rented sector*; Churches National Housing Coalition

Maclagan, I (1997) *Guide to training and benefits for young people*; Youthaid

Social Security Contributions and Benefits Act 1992

Chapter 9

Anglezarke, B (1996) 'Foyers in Wales: give us a chance!'; *Welsh Housing Quarterly*, Issue 23, pp 20-22

Chatrik, B (1997) *New Deal — Fair Deal? Black young people in the labour market*; Youthaid, The Children's Society, Barnados

Chauhan, V. (1997) The new treadmill; *Shabaab* No.21 August 1997

DfEE, Welsh Office, Scottish Office (1997) *Design of the New Deal for 18-24 year olds*

Duncan, P and Halsall, W (1995) *Don't forget the jobs: Housing associations and local economic development*; National Federation of Housing

Foyer Federation for Youth, Newsletter, Spring 1997

London Connection (1995) *Core skills training for homeless people*

McGregor, A et al (1997) *Bridging the jobs gap: An evaluation of the Wise Group and the intermediate labour market*; Joseph Rowntree Foundation

Simmonds, D et al (1997) *Making the New Deal work*; Training and Enterprise Network

Chapter 10

Brody, S (1997) *A few steps forward: Practical ways in which local authority provision for homeless 16 and 17-year-olds might be improved*; National Homeless Alliance

First Key (1996) *Standards in leaving care: Report of the national working group*

McCluskey, J (1994) *Acting in Isolation: An evaluation of the effectiveness of the Children Act for young homeless people*; CHAR

Whittaker, G (1993) 'Young black people leaving care: A continuing case of neglect', *Childright*, March 1993, No.94